Growing Up American

Immigrant Children in America
Then and Now

Twayne's History of American Childhood Series

Series Editors
Joseph M. Hawes, Memphis State University
N. Ray Hiner, University of Kansas

Growing Up American

Immigrant Children in America Then and Now

Selma Cantor Berrol

Twayne Publishers
An Imprint of Simon & Schuster Macmillan
New York
Prentice Hall International
London Mexico City New Delhi Singapore Sydney Toronto

Growing Up American: Immigrant Children in America, Then and Now
Selma Cantor Berrol

Copyright © 1995 by Twayne Publishers

Twayne Publishers
An Imprint of Simon & Schuster Macmillan
866 Third Avenue
New York, New York 10022

Library of Congress Cataloging-in-Publication Data

Berrol, Selma Cantor.
    Growing up American: immigrant children in America, then and now/Selma Cantor Berrol.
      p. cm.—(Twayne's history of American childhood series)
    Includes bibliographical references (p.) and index.
    ISBN 0-8057-4103-8.—ISBN 0-8057-4104-6 (pbk.)
    1. Children of immigrants—United States—History. 2. United States—Social life and cus-
toms. I. Title. II. Series.
E184.A1B429 1995
305.23'0973—dc20   94-24563
                                                                                                              CIP

The paper used in this publication meets the minimum requirements of American National Standard for Information Sciences—Permanence of Paper for Printed Library Materials, ANSI Z39.48-1984. ∞ ™

10 9 8 7 6 5 4 3 2 1 (hc)
10 9 8 7 6 5 4 3 2 1 (pbk)

Printed in the United States of America.

To my children, Philip and Ann,
and my granddaughter, Tracy,
all of whom are, to a greater or lesser degree,
the children of immigrants

Contents

Preface

This book is about immigrant children, defined as those who were born abroad or those born to immigrant parents within a few decades after their arrival in the United States. Although it may sound immodest to say so, I have excellent credentials for writing such a book. My parents were both emigrants from the czar's dominions. They met and married in Philadelphia early in the twentieth century, and I was their youngest child, born in 1924. As a result, I have experienced much of the good and bad that is described in this book.

Growing up is not easy for any child, but for those without American roots, it is even harder. I cannot claim to have endured the poverty that was the lot of so many immigrant children, because by the time I arrived my father had become the proprietor of a small paint store. Nor did I live in a tenement. Our quarters were a crowded four rooms above the store, which gradually became roomier as my siblings married and moved out. Furthermore, my neighborhood was not a ghetto but rather home to Italian, Irish, Jewish, and Polish families.

In spite of all these departures from the typical immigrant pattern, in other respects I, too, suffered from the immigrant child syndrome: derision, discrimination, confrontations with the neighborhood toughs, and, most of all, feelings of marginality. On the streets I contended with bigotry, in school Americanization, and the result was confusion. If I was not wanted, why should I try to be an American? Eventually, with strong support from my father, who valued his American citizenship as much as his wife, I opted for patriotism, as did most of the immigrant children of my generation. Because the pleasures and pains of growing up American were so much a part of my childhood, the history of American immigration became my major scholarly interest.

Many notable historians, such as Marcus Hansen, Oscar Handlin, Philip Taylor, and Carl Wittke, to mention just a few, have preceded me, and others, such as Thomas Kessner and Moses Rischin, are my contemporaries. In the course of using their excellent work, I noticed that children, per se, were not much noticed. One explanation for this is that for much of the twentieth century there was not much interest in social history, including such subjects as families and children. Beginning in the 1960s, however, a number of scholars turned their attention to the lives of ordinary people, and, among other subjects, the history of childhood emerged. Immigration historians, however, although also specializing in an area that had previously been subsumed in American history as a whole, did not attempt to connect the two new subdisciplines. This book is an attempt to fill the vacuum.

It is tempting to generalize about immigrants and their children, and, indeed, a number of myths have emerged from the oversimplification of complex matters. Hoping to avoid this pitfall, I have tried to keep in mind that the children who are the subject of this book were individuals and as such were as much shaped by differences in their gender, personality, and upbringing as by the experience of immigration. Time is another factor. Even for children from the same cultural background, when they were born or when they arrived in the United States affected their chances of basic survival as well as the nature of the opportunities that would be open to them.

Conditions in the larger society, such as child labor laws and the availability of public education, for example, exerted great influence on their lives. Location was still another modifier. Urban immigrants lived quite differently from their country cousins. Every state attracted some immigrants, but there was also a clear-cut pattern of preference. Statistics from the census of 1890 and 1910 show that Massachusetts and New York attracted the most Irish, Minnesota the most Swedes and Norwegians, and that Germans settled everywhere. When Russian Jews, Italians, and people from Austria-Hungary began to arrive, they made New York their first choice, with Illinois and Massachusetts competing for second place in their affections. Within these states, particular cities attracted particular groups. In Lawrence, Massachusetts, in 1890, for example, 38 percent of the population was Irish, and there were not enough Germans or any other group except French Canadians to appear in the statistics. In Milwaukee, on the other hand, 65 percent of the foreign-born were Scandinavians or Germans.

In spite of all the caveats, however, it is clear that the sons and daughters of foreign-born parents faced difficulties that the children whose families had stronger roots in American society did not. While the life of an Italian child who came to New York City in 1890 would not be the same as that of a German child who had come to Philadelphia 40 years earlier or a Dominican who flew to New York 60 years later, it is certain that the lives of all three would be quite different from those of the children who were part of families that had been here for many generations.

Because the differences between an Irish child coming to the New World on a sailing ship in 1850 and a Chinese youngster coming to San Francisco by plane in 1970 seem so enormous, historians have understandably found other aspects of the immigrant saga easier to study. In excellent surveys such as John Bodnar's *The Transplanted* (1985) or in valuable monographs such as Virginia Yans-McLaughlin's *Family and Community* (1982), the children of the immigrants are present but are not singled out for separate study. It is mostly in the collections of immigrant memoirs or interviews, such as *Our Parent's Lives* (1989), edited by Ruth and Neil Cowan, that the children's concerns are heard. My book is based on information from surveys, monographs, reminiscenses, and public data, all gathered for the purpose of constructing a picture of what it was—and is—like to be an immigrant child in America.

When I first planned the book I had intended to organize the material chronologically but I soon realized that such an approach required excessive repetition. Every immigrant child was confronted with the problem of adjusting to the demands of the new society while continuing to respect the language and culture of the old. Teachers, settlement workers, and other children pushed the newcomers to talk and act "American," while their parents demanded that they retain familiar language and customs. Some children obeyed the siren call of the schools and streets, while others stayed close to parents and home. Most, however, remained on the margins of both worlds.

Some parents accepted the reality of cultural discontinuity, understanding that if their children were to get ahead in the United States, they needed to become Americanized. Others, afraid that their children would be lost to them, forbade the use of English at home and tried to preserve as many Old World customs as possible. The resulting intergenerational conflict often led to rebellion, antisocial behavior, and family breakup. Sometimes it was the child who abandoned parents and siblings, rather than conform to traditional patterns. In other families it was the father who chose to leave home rather than remain in a situation where his authority was diminished. When this occurred, the poverty that afflicted so many immigrant children even when their father was present was deepened. Immigrant families were poor because employment opportunities were limited by discrimination, and wages, when they were hired, were low. This often meant that the children had to leave school to earn much needed money.

It seems clear that marginality, cultural discontinuity, and intergenerational conflict as well as poverty and discrimination, although modified by time, place, and ethnic group, were common to all and would, therefore, have to be discussed over and over again. Considering this, I decided on a topical approach in four chapters: the first brings the children to America and sees them through the settlement process, the second describes their schooling, the third their work and play, and the fourth discusses their relationships with their parents and the larger society. A fifth summary chapter draws comparisons between the groups who came before—Irish, German, Jewish, Indian—and the Asians and Caribbeans arriving now, stressing the differences between the experiences of immigrant children past and present. Within each chapter, I have followed a chronological approach, discussing the earliest arriving Irish and German children first, those from Southern and Eastern Europe next, and the newest arrivals from Asia and the Caribbean last.

The reader will quickly discover that some of the youngsters and their families get more attention than others. This is the result of an imbalance in the sources. More has been written about immigrants who settled in urban areas, more on those who arrived between 1880 and 1920, least on the newest groups, who are still arriving. I've tried to touch, if not completely cover, all the bases; for those who want to dig deeper, there is an extensive bibliography.

Acknowledgments

The New York Public Library holds an enormous amount of material related to the subject of this book. I appreciate both the volumes it holds and the courtesy of the staff in making it possible for me to use the Wertheim Room and the services it provides. I also wish to thank Professors Ray Hiner and Joseph Hawes for inviting me to be a part of this series on American childhood.

1

Starting In, Making Do

Children were present from the first years of settlement in all of the colonies established on the Atlantic coast of what was to become the United States. Small faces, framed by bonnets or topped by overlarge hats, appear in paintings and are mentioned in records left by the earliest arrivals who came from Holland, the various German states, France, Sweden, and the British Isles in the seventeenth century. In many cases the children were part of a community of like-minded people, such as Puritans in Massachusetts Bay or Quakers in Pennsylvania, and therefore not likely to experience the nativism that later arrivals had to face. In other respects, however, their experiences were similar to those of the immigrants who came during the next three centuries.

Regardless of their time of arrival or their cultural or geographical background, children who emigrated with their parents in every period of American history suffered trauma from the loss of a familiar place, harsh conditions of travel, difficulties of finding food and shelter, dangerous illnesses, and the possibility of losing one or both parents. Those born to immigrant parents in the United States escaped the first two hazards, but they, too, faced poverty, illness, and loss. The difficulties were greater for some than others. In the seventeenth century, English colonists and their children traveling on sailing ships were in greater danger than the Italians coming on steamships two centuries later; Jews escaping the czar's dominions had to make a long and dangerous land trip before they embarked; most Swedes and Norwegians faced an arduous inland trip after they landed in America; and many of the members of every group received, at best, a tepid welcome.

The latest arrivals from Asia, coming by air, have had an easier time getting here. This is not equally true for many of the most desperate coming from the Caribbean, such as the Haitians and Cubans, who travel by whatever means they can find and as a result have been in greater danger than most of the Europeans who preceded them. Legal barriers to entry have faced all the immigrants coming to America since the late eighteenth century, but they are higher for those coming from the Caribbean, Central America, and Africa today.

Variables of time, place, and ethnicity appear to separate immigrant children and make generalizations difficult. If we focus solely on the details of their lives, this is an accurate perception. But if we examine the broader aspects of their experience—arrival, settlement, and survival—we see how much all immigrant children, past and present, have in common. That is what this chapter will begin to do.

Arrival

Children who arrived in the New World from Europe in the late seventeenth and eighteenth centuries endured an ocean trip lasting two to six months. Most of the German, Dutch, and Sephardic Jewish immigrants left from Rotterdam or Amsterdam; the Welsh, the Irish, the Scots, and the Swedes departed from British ports. The cost of passage was cheaper for children than for adults. On British ships, suckling babies traveled free and children younger than five were charged 50 shillings; their parents were charged £5 each.[1]

Conditions aboard the sailing ships were horrible. They were frequently becalmed and often sprung leaks; some were boarded by pirates who left the passengers bereft of whatever valuables that had brought to help them start a new life. Rations were limited by shipowners' greed and by spoilage, especially when the voyage took longer than expected. As a result of the poor nutrition, crowding, and disease, many immigrants, young and old, did not live to see the New World. As one traveler observed: "Betwixt decks, there can hardlie a man fetch his breath by reason there arises a funke in the night that it causes putrification of the blood and breedeth disease much like the plague." In 1711, when conditions were somewhat improved over the preceding century, "of a total of 3,086 immigrants who embarked, 859 died en-route or immediately after." Fearing contagion, the proprietors of Pennsylvania, the favored landing place of new arrivals, forbade any ship carrying infected passengers from coming closer than one mile. They purchased land for a pesthouse in Philadelphia, which was the busiest immigrant port until 1825. In that year New York took first place, because the opening of the Erie Canal made access to the West easier.[2]

A large proportion of the new arrivals were redemptioners or indentured servants, people too poor to pay the costs of travel and thus prepared to work as servants for three to seven years to earn the money advanced for the journey by the shipowner. Children were a part of this group. Most came with their families, but some Irish youngsters arrived alone, homeless or neglected children who been shipped out from Great Britain to ease the drain on funds for the poor. In any case, at the port of entry, individuals or an entire family were offered to the highest bidder.

Families were often split up, with children going to one employer and their parents to another. As a German observer reported: "Many parents must sell and trade away their children like so many head of cattle, for if the children take the debt upon themselves, the parents can leave the ship free and unrestrained; but as the parents often do not know where and to what people their children are going, it often happens to such parents and children after leaving the ship do not see each other for many years, perhaps no more in all of their lives."[3]

When they had completed their terms of service, some parents placed messages in newspapers hoping to find the children they had lost. Because indentured children were usually required to serve until they were 21 and might be living anywhere, reunion was difficult to arrange. During the years of their indenture, most learned a trade that stood them in good stead when they were freed, but there is little evidence to indicate that they received any formal education. Except in New England, schools were few and primarily for religious training.[4]

Seventeenth- and eighteenth-century immigrants settled in all the colonies, but certain groups chose specific locations for specific reasons. New Amsterdam, of course, was the choice of the Dutch and also of the French Huguenots who emigrated after the Edict of Nantes was revoked in 1685. Pietistic groups, refugees from the Palatinate, Welsh Quakers, and Germans chose Pennsylvania. The frontier that ran from New York to Virginia attracted the Scots-Irish, the largest group of non-English immigrants to arrive in the seventeenth century. Jews went to Rhode Island because it was the most tolerant of the colonies; Swedes went to Delaware, where the flag of their homeland flew until first the Dutch and then the British took control.[5]

As a result of the immigration that had taken place from 1619 to the outbreak of the American Revolution in 1776, the population of the colonies that were soon to become the United States of America was basically Anglo-Saxon. But important non-English elements, most of whom came in the eighteenth century, were present as well, establishing a pattern that was to persist for the next three centuries. Attracted by advertising placed in English, French, German, and Dutch periodicals by proprietors such as William Penn and shipowners looking for paying customers, thousands of Europeans, unhappy with religious persecution, heavy taxes, and land shortages and optimistic about the possibilities of a better life in the new world, began to see the American colonies as the promised land. Worried about too great an exodus, the British government forbade the emigration of skilled workers as early as 1660; but it never seriously enforced the law, and artisans continued to leave in sizable numbers.[6]

There was a temporary decline in arrivals between 1790 and 1820. Uncertainty about the new government established after the Revolution in 1789 made America less attractive, and in 1798 the first restrictions on immigration were approved by a Federalist Congress wanting to keep out revolutionary French and destitute Irish who might support the Jeffersonian Republicans. In spite of the decline, however, when the federal government first counted immigrant heads, in 1820, it found that 8,385 people who had been born elsewhere had entered the new United States in the previous decade. In the next 10 years, 143,439 arrived, a figure that doubled in the following 10 years and between 1851 and 1861, when the outbreak of the Civil War dammed the flow, 2.5 million men, women, and children arrived in the New World. Many more, of course, were to come during the period of expansion that followed the war.[7]

Irish immigrants made up a large proportion of those who came before the Civil War. The Irish children and adults who arrived in the 1840s and 1850s landed at the port cities on the East Coast, most often New York and Boston. Some had been "shoveled out" of Ireland, along with their parents, to relieve the burden of feeding them. In most cases they were very poor and had suffered terribly on the voyage across the Atlantic. For some this had followed a two-day trip across the Irish Sea on the top deck of a small boat with no amenities. Goods and livestock took precedence over people: "passengers were packed shoulder to shoulder, drenched with spray with access to only one water pump on a deck that was afloat with animal mire." This unpleasant beginning of their journey was undertaken to reach Liverpool, from whence a ship would take them to New York. Their alternative was to embark from an Irish port, such as Dublin or Belfast, Londonderry or Cork, and arrive, after a longer trip, at Quebec, Philadelphia, or New Orleans. Other emigrants from the British Isles, except for the Scots-Irish leaving Ulster, had an easier time reaching Liverpool, the port that offered the best chance for a speedy departure.[8]

On a typical voyage in the 1840s and 1850s, in all kinds of weather they were confined to steerage, where the maximum height of the cabin was five feet, a problem for adolescents and adults. In stormy weather, conditions grew worse because the hatches were battened down, leaving the passengers, young and old, "buried in darkness and stench." There was "no where to hang clothes, no where to eat in comfort." There was also little to do, and "monotony was a feature of all crossings." Children found the cramped life extremely difficult. Even when the weather permitted them to go on deck, the area was too crowded to permit the kind of exercise they needed. Sometimes they helped the crew, sometimes they played marbles, cards, and dominoes, and sometimes they picked quarrels (especially Irish versus Welsh) and got their exercise that way.[9]

Hunger was a serious problem. Most families brought food with them but found that it was soon inedible, and the ship's provisions were almost always inadequate. In 1850, 12 Irish children died of starvation on one ship from Liverpool, and on many more of the ships in the immigrant trade others died of ship's fever brought on by inadequate rations. Young children were especially vulnerable to disease and accidents. In 1860, even on a well-regulated ship, 20 children died for every adult. Cholera was a major cause of death for children and adults, especially for Germans who embarked from Hamburg, a major departure point attracting thousands of people, who had already traveled extensively across Europe to get there.

Cholera, an infectious gastrointestinal disease carried by human and animal waste, appeared in many European towns and cities in the seventeenth, eighteenth, and nineteenth centuries. Given the primitive conditions an emigrant family would encounter on their way to port, infection was a strong possibility. In 1853 inspectors in New York found that 21 percent of the ships from Liverpool, 25 percent of those from London, and 33 percent of the ships from Hamburg had cholera cases aboard. In truth, no one was exempt from illness. The sailing ships on which the nineteenth-century immigrant traveled were overcrowded and lacked adequate ventilation. Too many people in too small a space, especially when a storm stirred up the accumulated filth, led to epidemics of typhus, smallpox, and dysentery as well as cholera.[10]

The most destitute of the children who came to Boston had traveled on open timber ships that first touched land in Quebec. In company with their parents, sometimes on foot, they made their way to Boston, a city that Oscar Handlin said was the most inhospital place for them to settle because it "had no room for strangers." Culturally homogeneous, Protestant to the core, lacking space to expand in economic as well as physical terms, new poor and Catholic arrivals would have been well advised to go elsewhere. Many did come to New York, where they were somewhat more likely to be accepted and passed through Castle Garden, an immigrant receiving center established by New York State in 1855.[11]

Prior to that date, the often sick and destitute immigrants (more often Irish than members of other groups coming to America in the middle of the nineteenth century, such as Germans and Scandinavians) "received meagre assistance, if any," from inadequate private organizations or neglectful city officials. All the port cities had benevolent societies to aid the worthy poor, founded in the eighteenth century by wealthy merchants and professionals. Some focused on the immigrant poor but most did not, leaving the task to groups organized along ethnic and religious lines, such as the Friendly Sons of St. Patrick and the German Benevolent Society. After passage of a New York State Immigration Act in 1847, however, the Board of Commissioners of Emigration, consisting of representatives of the city government, as well as the German Society and the Irish Emigrant Society, made arrival some-what easier.[12]

The board, however, was unable to cope with some of the worst problems because most of the new arrivals, sick or well, scattered after landing and became victims of "runners" who cheated and stole from them. Clearly, a landing point for all ships containing immigrants was badly needed, but attempts to lease a pier were blocked by an injunction obtained by nearby residents who "feared inconvenience and lowered property values." It took five years to overcome opposition, but once opened, Castle Garden, just off the tip of Manhattan Island, formerly part of the city's fortifications and more recently a place of amusement, became the landing depot for immigrants and their children. It was a much needed improvement.[13]

At Castle Garden new arrivals could change money, buy railroad tickets, write letters, and deposit valuables while they looked for permanent shelter. They also met representatives of church groups, charitable organizations, and employment agencies. Perhaps most important to the Germans and other non-English-speaking newcomers, there were interpreters. Before receiving any of the services, however, new arrivals of all ages were required to take a much needed bath. There were two sex-separated washrooms, each one 20 by 25 feet, with a bathtub large enough for 12 people and a trough that permitted them to stand and scrub. Attendants supervised the process, giving out towels and forcing the bathers to use soap. No other port city had anything like Castle Garden and its baths.[14]

Wherever they first set foot on dry land, the immigrants and their children were sorted out according to their physical and mental condition and degree of dependency. In New York, adults diagnosed as insane or found to be destitute were sent along with their children to a hospital on Ward's Island. So were sick children, who when they were well enough could attend the primary school on the premises. If they were healthy and part of an intact family or, best of all, met by a relative who had immigrated earlier, children were free to leave Castle Garden soon. Other children, alone because their parents had died en route or, like thousands of immigrants young and old, had died in American hospitals shortly after arrival, were ushered into various forms of care. Irish or German Catholic orphans were transferred to a Catholic institution or foster home. Non-Catholic youngsters would be sent to Protestant institutions or foster families.[15]

In New York, in 1817, a Roman Catholic Orphan Asylum was opened in an old wooden shanty where 28 Irish children were cared for by nuns. Owing to the disruption of family life by illness, death, and desertion in the growing Irish population, the Diocese had to open two more orphanages by

1830. Fifteen years later there were 350 boys and girls in these institutions, in 1859 there were 500, and even more after the Civil War. This was also the pattern in Boston, where after 1833 destitute Irish girls were taken to St. Vincent's Orphan Asylum, also staffed by nuns.

In New York, beginning in 1851, boys were cared for by monks at the House of the Guardian Angel and, after 1864, at the Home for Destitute Catholic Children. German Catholics opened their own orphanage in New York in 1850 because the cholera epidemic of the previous year had left so many children without parents. In all the East Coast port cities, cholera thrived best in places with poor drainage and ventilation, usually the areas in which the Irish lived; the population of Catholic orphanages swelled with every cholera epidemic.[16]

After 1860, thanks to the efforts of the existing German Jewish community, there was also a place for Jewish orphans in New York City. The German Jewish effort had been stimulated by the fact that some of their orphans were being placed in Catholic or Protestant institutions. Fear of losing children through conversion led the established Jewish community to enlarge the work of the United Hebrew Charities and, with help from the municipal government, establish the Hebrew Orphan Asylum. Before that date, most Jewish orphans who did not become part of a family would be sent to Protestant institutions, which were more likely to have funds.[17]

The Catholic community found it difficult to spare money or staff for orphans; indeed, Archbishop John Hughes had to import six Sisters of Charity from Ireland to care for orphaned immigrant girls. Conditions in all the orphanages, Catholic, Protestant, or Jewish, that sheltered immigrant children, left much to be desired. None of the sponsors had much money and therefore had to cut corners whenever they could. In the Cleveland, Ohio, Jewish Orphan Asylum, the children were always hungry and "engaged in a relentless struggle for food, stealing from the kitchen or from other children." When institutional space ran out and foster homes in the port cities were unavailable, orphaned children of all faiths were sometimes forced to move again, this time to rural areas where it was assumed they would be less likely to become thieves or prostitutes.[18]

Coming to a strange big city, even with parents and siblings, was quite a shock to the young newcomers, most of whom had spent their earlier years in rural communities. Weak, tired, dirty after a lengthy and difficult trip from home to their new destination, frightened, and insecure, the Irish, German, and Scandinavian parents and children who debarked from the sailing ships that had brought them across the Atlantic were a sorry lot and received little help at the ports of Boston and Philadelphia and not enough at Castle Garden.

Furthermore, for many, landing in a port city did not mean the end of the journey. Irish families arriving in New York often took a steamboat to

Fall River, Massachusetts, or some other New England industrial city, while Scandinavians and Germans embarked on a route that took them to the Midwest via the Hudson River, the Erie Canal, or rail. Those landing at Philadelphia followed the Lancaster Turnpike toward the West. Some well-informed Germans who were bound for the Midwest debarked at New Orleans and used the Mississipi River and its tributaries to reach their destination.[19]

Inland travel, although not as dangerous to the immigrants and their children as the ocean crossing, also presented hazards. To begin with, long waits and discomforts at crowded railroad depots created much anxiety in people who did not understand English. Once on the train, "crowded and caged," the journey seemed endless. One nine-year-old Norwegian girl recalled a trip in 1864 that took her family by canalboat and train to Grand Haven, by another boat across Lake Michigan to Milwaukee, and by one more train across Wisconsin before final settlement in Iowa.[20]

This much-traveled child was following in the footsteps of earlier Scandinavians. The sloop *Restauration* had sailed from Stavenger, Norway, in 1825 with 53 pilgrims bound for the United States. A small group of Quakers followed five years later, beginning a movement that brought thousands of Swedes and Norwegians to the United States after the Civil War. An old emigrant song explains why they left:

> Farewell, thou Mother Norway. Now I must leave thee
> All too sparing wast thou in providing food for
> the throng of thy laborers, though thou gavest
> more than enough to thy well schooled sons.

Quebec became an important port for debarkation for Scandinavians after the British Parliament repealed the Navigation Acts in 1849, making it possible for shipowners to replace the emigrants they had brought to North America with Canadian lumber on the return trip and thereby lower passenger fares.[21]

For most of these Northern European immigrants, the flat, unbroken land in the Midwest on which they hoped to settle under the terms of the Homestead Act was the end of a very long trip. The heroine of O. E. Rolvaag's *Giants in the Earth* (1927) described her family's journey from Norway to America: from native village via a small coastal boat to the seaport of Namsos and a two-month trip across the Atlantic to Quebec followed by further travel by horse and wagon to the village of Detroit, then farther to Milwaukee, and finally, a seemingly endless trip to South Dakota. Other Norwegians became city dwellers. Chicago was seen as the gateway to the West, and while most Scandinavians passed through, enough remained there to form a community in the Humboldt Park area. Other cities in the Midwest that attracted them included Minneapolis and Duluth in Minnesota, La Crosse and Eau Claire,

Wisconsin, Sioux City, Iowa, and Fargo, North Dakota. There were also settle-ments near Seattle, Washington, where they "felt at home with the opportuni-ties in fishing and shipping." Early settlements back East, such as Fox River in Illinois, acted as "mother colonies" from which the pioneers moved on to break new ground farther west. A woman who made such a trek on foot remembered carrying small children over rivers and creeks.[22]

Some aspects of arrival and settlement were equally traumatic for the young Italians, Poles, and Russian Jews who entered the United States between 1880 and 1914. For many of these immigrants the trip had been long awaited. The father, unable to raise enough money to buy ship tickets for the entire family, often left home first. In most cases he worked, saved, sent money home, and wrote regularly, but when this did not happen, his wife and children were left to fend for themselves and were most unhappy. When the months after Leonard Covello's father left had stretched into a year and his letters had stopped coming, Leonard pestered his mother with anxious questions. The poor woman, herself in great distress, told him to watch for a butterfly in the house. If one entered, it would mean that they would soon get "news from father and it will be news that he is sending for us." Young Leonardo, hoping to hasten the advent of the good news, caught a butterfly and let it loose in the house. Perhaps this did the trick; steamship tickets arrived not long after.[23]

In the main, the immigrants from southern Italy and Eastern Europe had the better experience. For one thing, their voyage was made on a steamship that usually took only 12 days from a Western European port, and for anoth-er, governmental regulations had forced the shipping companies into provid-ing somewhat better conditions, even in the lowest category, steerage. There were fewer berths, although still two tiers of them, and there was now a cen-tral area with tables and chairs. Toilets were inconveniently located, but there were more of them. There were, however, no opportunities for bathing, and in general the quarters were still crowded and dirty. As one aged woman who had come as a child remembered, the food consisted mostly of herring and potatoes.

The voyage was not easy for any of the migrants, but individual stories make it clear that it was more difficult for some than others. On a ship trav-eling from Bremen in 1903, a 16-year-old Russian Jewish girl was responsi-ble for a younger sister, twin eight-year-old brothers, a three-year-old boy, and a two-month-old infant boy. Her mother had died during his birth, and her father, who had immigrated to Philadelphia earlier, sent her steamship tickets and instructions for bringing over the whole family. The newly born child had been fed by a wet nurse in his first weeks and could not adjust to the cow's milk, which was all his big sister could give him. In desperation, she searched for a nursing mother among her fellow passengers, found sev-eral, and baby Max survived the journey.[24]

As photographs taken at the point of debarkation show, the immigrant families arriving two or three decades after the Irish and Germans were as tired and frightened as earlier arrivals had been. Some had made a long overland trip to Hamburg or Naples, crossed borders by stealth, and experienced much hostility en route. Government officials in France and Germany were afraid that the needy arrivals from Eastern Europe, Sicily, and southern Italy would if treated well remain and become a burden to the community.

In Western Europe generally, anti-Semites and those who wanted to keep their native population free of foreign influences were not welcoming. In addition, earlier arrivals, such as German Jews and northern Italians, were afraid that their newly arrived kinsmen would attract unwanted nativist attention to them. To avoid such difficulties, all the concerned groups, public and private, did their best to keep the immigrants moving out of continental Europe and on to Great Britain or the United States. The British, however, also had no desire to enlarge their population with destitute foreigners and encouraged them to cross the Atlantic as soon as possible.

One immigrant child barely made it to the ship. He and his parents, like many emigrants, left Russia as part of a group. Just at the point that they were trying to cross the German border without attracting the attention of the frontier guards, who would, at the very least, demand a bribe for allowing them to leave Russia and enter Germany, he began to cry loudly, thereby endangering 20 people, some of whom suggested suffocating him for the common good.[25]

The border between Russia and Germany was the site of a control station where the emigrants had to pass a medical inspection and have their baggage fumigated. Girls and older women with long hair sometimes had their heads shaved to prevent the spread of hair lice. Mary Antin, who made a 16-day sea voyage across the Atlantic in 1894, remembered the border crossings into Germany being the most troublesome part of her voyage to America. The Antin family was found free of lice after examination, but the German authorities, accustomed to extorting money from immigrants passing through, demanded payment from their near-penniless mother. A representative of a German Jewish emigrant aid society came to the rescue to keep the Antins moving on to the seaport city of Hamburg.[26]

This was the pattern followed by most of the emigrants from Eastern Europe. After the necessary bribes had been paid and neither they nor their belongings were found to be infectious, they were loaded into a railroad car for a trip to Hamburg or Bremen. If their destination was the former port, and they had a little money, they were in for a pleasant surprise. In 1903, the Hamburg-American steamship line had established an emigrant village that provided good services at reasonable fees; there was even a band that played twice a day, which surely must have pleased the children. Italian youngsters had a less pleasant experience at their customary port of embarkation, Naples, where, in addition to the usual medical examination and baggage fumigation, they were required to have an unfamiliar and terrifying smallpox vaccination.[27]

One youngster did not see Hamburg when the rest of her family did because she was suffering from trachoma, a serious form of conjunctivitis, and her parents were aware that the ailment would prevent her admission to the United States. She was forced to see her entire family leave Poland while she remained with relatives until her eyes improved. With the help of an agent, she made the trip to New York a year later. In another variant, when there was not enough money to bring a whole family to America, the father took the oldest child, usually a son, who could earn money to help bring over the mother and the younger siblings.[28]

Although the trip was still an ordeal, the years that had elapsed since the Irish and Germans had come to America in large numbers had made a difference. For one thing, the north German shipping lines most used by those leaving Russia and Poland had been forced by the British and American governments to establish screening procedures among their steerage passengers before embarkation. As a result, there were fewer critically ill arrivals and fewer orphaned children. For another, the port cities, especially New York, were better equipped to process the newcomers. In the 1880s Russian and Polish Jewish immigrants of all ages were less likely to be robbed or led astray because the established German Jewish community had formed efficient organizations, such as the Hebrew Immigrant Aid Society (HIAS), whose representatives met the newcomers at the dock. The society, organized in 1909, was an amalgam of two groups, the Hebrew Sheltering Society and an earlier immigrant aid group, and soon became the most important helping agency for the immigrant Jewish poor.[29]

Finally, Ellis Island, which opened in 1891, was a much better receiving station than Castle Garden. For most families, other than the nuisance of a physical examination and the long lines in which to wait in order to be interviewed and cleared, the procedures were relatively painless. As one young boy told a friend, "If you are allright in every way, you go through very quickly." Other youngsters may not have had such an easy time. According to Bertha Boody, a psychologist who was testing incoming children's intelligence (with a view to excluding imbeciles and idiots as prescribed by federal law), for most, it was a "time of tension."[30]

If any member of a family was found to be unhealthy, for example, the group was seen as incomplete and had to go to a special waiting room until the officials told them whether the ailing or incompetent member, child or adult, could stay or would have to go back to Europe. If it was a child who required medical care, he or she would be sent to the hospital maintained at Ellis Island. A mother would not be able to see her little boy or girl until the next day. One can easily imagine the child's terror and the parents' anguish over the separation.[31]

Boody also indicated that such a separation was often a mistake, because children were often "hungry and fretful," not really sick, when the overworked doctors examined them. Moreover, the examination itself was often imperfect, leading the professionals to see a child as a medical problem when he or she, frightened and tired, cried long and hard. Mistakes were also made on the mental examination. A Greek boy, aged eight, was detained when he seemed unable to count from 1 to 20. When his parents found an interpreter to administer the test, however, the result was quite different. Less frightened, the youngster sailed through the test "without difficulty."[32]

There were still other reasons for detaining children. One large family, for example, was unable to pay the $25-per-child fee required at Ellis Island and had to leave a 12-year-old daughter behind, "in dirt and amidst terrible smells," until HIAS was able to telegraph relatives in Chicago who sent enough money to "bail" her out. The case was not unique; so many children were detained at Ellis Island that authorities maintained a school for them. Some were waiting for a parent or a sibling to recover from an illness that had led to hospitalization, some expected a relative from another city to come and claim them, some had arrived under false pretenses, that is, with an adult who was not, as claimed, his or her biological or adopted parent. The school was voluntary, but many of the "older" children (aged 10–14), especially girls, did attend. Others, especially those with a contagious disease such as trachoma, were not permitted to go to school and endured the discomforts and loneliness of the island's hospital ward only to be deported when the doctors decided that he or she could not be cured in a reasonable period of time. In at least one case, a child who was about to be deported was so terrified at the thought of separation that her mother left the rest of the family and returned to Europe with her.[33]

The "Island of Tears," as some labeled Ellis Island, was a busy place until the outbreak of World War I, during which it became a military base as well as a detention center for aliens under suspicion of committing sabotage or of being opposed to the war. It was even busier after the war ended. Ships bearing refugees from war-damaged Europe and escaping the chaos of the Russian Revolution were anchored in New York Bay as far as the eye could see. Fearing a deluge, in 1917 Congress passed a Literacy Act that required adult immigrants to read and write in some language, but it did little to stem the flow. In 1921, therefore, Congress passed a restrictive act that assigned quotas based on the population of foreign national groups living in the United States as of 1910. Each year no more than 3 percent of each group's U.S. population was to be allowed enter. Three years later, the base year was moved back to 1890, when fewer of the immigrants from Southern and Eastern Europe would have been living here, and the quota was lowered to 2 percent. Thus refined and strengthened, the National Origins Act had the desired effect, and in 1929 Ellis Island closed its doors.[34]

Angel Island in California was another place that saw its share of tears. Before it opened in 1910, the comparatively small number of immigrants entering the United States in San Francisco were detained in a shed at the waterfront. The construction of a new station on a small island in San Francisco Bay was part of the effort of the federal government to restrict Chinese immigration as Congress had intended to do when it passed the Chinese Exclusion Act in 1882. New arrivals were given stringent medical examinations and "closely interrogated for one or two hours" to see if they were eligible for entry. Many of the applicants were young boys, aged 10–15, who claimed to be the sons of Chinese American citizens. Some were, but others were merely "paper sons," using false documents to prove eligibility. One, Jim Quock, remembered buying a "citizen paper" for $102 in gold in China and enduring endless questions when he got to Angel Island. He had prepared answers while still in China, but couldn't be sure that the preparation would get him through.

While waiting for admission, Quock and other detainees were held in locked barracks separated by sex and containing double- and triple-tiered beds. There was no privacy in the bathrooms, "where non-partitioned toilets lined the walls." The questioning took three weeks and was designed to see if the purported son's answers agreed with the information given by the purported father. After a fire in 1940, Angel Island was closed and Chinese detainees were moved to other places in San Francisco.[35]

These "Heartbreak Hotels," as some saw them, disappeared with the advent of air transportation. International airports in New York and San Francisco, not piers, are likely to be the first stop for the Chinese, Japanese, Korean, and other Asian families who have dominated American immigration statistics since the late 1960s. This is also true for emigrés from Russia and other areas of Eastern Europe who are joining their Americanized countrymen and -women. Miami International Airport serves the same function for those who emigrate from Central America or the Caribbean.[36]

Children, of course, are part of this varied movement of people to America, just as they were in the past. Today, however, their arrival is quite different from that of the boys and girls who preceded them. Today's children, Haitians and Cubans excepted, have a shorter and easier trip and do not experience the same anxieties upon arrival as did the foreign-born youngsters who preceded them because most of the inspection and interrogation has been done by U.S. consular officials prior to emigration. As a result, most children's stay in the terminal is relatively brief. In general, immigration procedures are simpler, and most newcomers are certain to be met by a close relative because it is the family reunion provision of the 1965 act that has enabled them to emigrate at all. Up to 1991, when the cold war ended, Cubans and Soviet Jews came as refugees with the assistance of the U.S. government, which was acting out of anticommunist sentiment. Likewise,

Cambodian and Vietnamese refugees were accepted because their parents had survived a war in which the United States played a large part. They were met by representatives of organizations such as the New York Association for New Americans (NYANA) and, in a number of ways, their introduction has been easier than it was for immigrants who arrived earlier.[37]

Even without the help of the government, social agencies, or kinfolk, the children of the newest arrivals are generally able to make a more comfortable adjustment to America because they are "members of a generation that knows the American world from television and movies" and therefore do not experience the culture shock that was the lot of their predecessors. Children who arrive without papers are likely to be interned and are often deported. They are informed about the United States, but their preconceived ideas do not fit the reality that awaits them when they arrive. They and their parents have tried and failed to enter the United States as refugees and have been kept in detention while their appeals are decided. Other young immigrants have eluded capture and may be among the many undocumented children—hundreds of thousands, according to some estimates—living in various urban areas. Many do not go to school because their parents fear that the family's illegal status will be revealed and that they will be deported.[38]

The Basics: Shelter and Food

Having overcome the hazards and discomforts of arrival, immigrant families, then and now, need to find a place to live. Many, especially the Irish who came to New York, did not travel far from the docks. Most moved into housing in the Sixth and Seventh Wards in Lower Manhattan. As was to happen time and again, the older residents moved out when the poor and newly arrived Irish moved in, and as a result the newcomers soon constituted a majority. Most lived in old houses converted into tenements by putting up partitions for three or more families or, when that supply was exhausted, in small apartments without much light or air. Population density increased quickly, as each shipload discharged immigrant families seeking shelter. In the Seventh Ward, "the average block density rose from 54.5 persons per acre in 1820 to 170.9 in 1840." As a result of the crowding, the wards were "hotbeds of diseases peculiar to children."[39]

The Irish child whose family settled in Boston did not live in better housing than his or her peers in New York. The buildings in South Boston, the center of Irish settlement in the 1850s, were also overcrowded tenements, three to six stories high, with poor light and inadequate ventilation. As a result, the death rate among Irish children in Boston and elsewhere was "alarmingly high." There were similar "Little Dublins" in the factory towns of New England and the Mid-Atlantic states where working-class Irish immigrants settled.[40]

Few German immigrants came to New England, but many chose to stay in New York where their children grew up in an immigrant enclave, the Tenth Ward on the far East Side of Manhattan. Housing in "Kleinedeutschland," as it was soon dubbed, was also quite poor. The district contained the same tenements and dark-"railroad" flats (only one room had windows) as the Irish neighborhoods on the West Side.[41] A good many of the German children whose parents had chosen to emigrate to America, however, had a better chance at a decent home, because their parents opted to leave the crowded East Coast cities for other areas in the Mid-Atlantic states, such as Pennsylvania. Those whose mothers and fathers chose to settle in the Midwest were probably going to live in farmhouses that might be crude and uncomfortable but less densely packed. This was also true for the Swedish and Norwegian children arriving at the same time—the 1860s–1880s—whose parents almost always left the city to farm the land.

According to O. E. Rolvaag, the first step taken by the Norwegians who chose to settle on the prairies where no other Europeans had been was to set up a tent that held their supplies and had room for two beds, one for the parents and the other for the children. Cooking and eating were done outside as long as the weather permitted. Some families, unwilling to live on a dirt floor, set up temporary housing in the bed of the wagon that had brought them west. It was, of course, essential to have more permanent housing before winter, but there was an equally great need to plow and plant in order to have food during that winter. Torn by conflicting needs, the children were usually sent to prepare the soil and plant the seeds while their parents built a sod house.[42]

Although Hamlin Garland, unlike Rolvaag, was not part of an immigrant family, as a youngster his living conditions were quite similar to that of the Scandinavian families who settled in the Midwest. As he described in his memoir, *A Son of the Middle Border* (1962), when his parents had been able to leave their primitive sod house, he lived in "an unpainted square cottage" that provided a sitting room and bedroom for his parents on the first floor while the children slept in a "low, unplastered chamber" overhead. This loft was warmed only by a stovepipe, which in winter led the youngsters to make a dash to the 16-foot-square kitchen at the front of the building. The kitchen was warmed by a large stove and became the "heart of house."[43] Another early settler, who left Norway with 13 children, settled at Pine Lake, Wisconsin, and built a house that "consisted of a living room, kitchen and dining room, two small upper rooms and a little clothing closet." One wonders where he put the 13 children.[44]

For the thousands of Italian families who disembarked in New York City after 1880, the wilderness and farming held little appeal. Most joined the

Russian Polish and Galician Jews who also had no taste for agriculture and small-town living in repeopling the lower districts of Manhattan. Italian children lived in buildings previously inhabited by the Irish, who by the latter decades of the nineteenth century were able to move uptown to slightly better housing in Hell's Kitchen, a district on the West Side of Manhattan above Forty-second Street. The same process occurred in Kleinedeutschland, where Jewish youngsters filled the schools that had previously held German boys and girls. Coming later, however, meant that the housing built or renovated for earlier immigrants had deteriorated. As a result, many of the latecomers lived under even worse conditions than those who had preceded them.[45]

Others, however, benefited from arriving from the 1890s onward because New York City housing laws then specified that light, air, and toilets (albeit communal) be available in any new housing that was constructed. To meet these legal requirements, "dumbell" tenements, which admitted somewhat more air and light by means of an airshaft, were built. Such apartments consisted of a front parlor, a kitchen, and two small bedrooms, separated from a rear apartment by the air shaft. Two toilets were tucked into the space around the shaft to service the residents of the four apartments on each floor.[46]

Crowding persisted, however, partly because relatives from the old country frequently arrived with no place to stay and partly because boarders were needed to help pay the rent. Harry Roskolenko, who in 1907 lived in a tenement with a toilet in the hall, said that he was afraid to go to school because when he came home a stranger would have his bed and he would be exiled to a pallet on the kitchen floor. His fear was not unreasonable. In the same period, Jacob Riis visited a tenement apartment and found that "the only bed was occupied by most of an immigrant family lying lengthwise and crosswise . . . all except a boy of twelve for whom there was no room. He slept, with his clothes on to keep warm, in pile of rags just inside the door." Another contemporary observer described the living conditions in a New York City Russian Jewish apartment in this way: "A family consisting of a husband, wife and six to eight children whose ages range from one to twenty five live under the following conditions. The parents occupy the original small bedroom together with two, three or even four of their younger children. In the kitchen, on cots or on the floor, are the older children, in the front room two or more lodgers sleep on the floor or on cots."[47]

Ethnicity made little difference in crowding. In 1901 in a Polish neighborhood in Chicago or an Italian one in Philadelphia a child might share a two- or three-room apartment with parents, grandparents, siblings, boarders, and cousins. Leonard Covello recalled living in a crowded apartment in the East Harlem area of New York, where he slept with two of his brothers in one bed. There was a water pump and a toilet in the hall for the use of the inhabitants of four apartments. Many of Philadelphia's Italian immigrant families had to cook, eat, and sleep in the same room and shared a privy and a water hydrant with four or five other families.

An immigrant child who spent his early years in the Italian district of New York recalled living "in a small, short alley called Extra Place near the Bowery and First Street." The toilets "were made of cast iron and were [located] in the halls."[48] Philadelphia's Jewish settlers lived in "blocks of old and unimproved row houses" that were no more comfortable than apartments in the multistory tenements rented by poor families in New York. One of the many surveys taken by Philadelphia reformers showed that in one three-room house, "sixteen persons slept in two rooms, 8x10x7." In spite of the fact that these houses were old and inadequate, the immigrant children who lived there entered and left them via stone steps that were scrubbed daily and were the pride of the neighborhood.[49]

Although electricity and steam heat were available by 1900, few immigrant children experienced such comforts. Kerosene was used for lighting. Some apartments were equipped to use gas for illumination and cooking but it cost 25 cents per hour by meter and was used only on special occasions. Coal, therefore, was usually the fuel of choice and since heat was the responsibility of the tenant, coal was a major expense. Louis Lefkowitz said that when there was no money for coal, he and his brothers would "make a truck out of a fruit crate with wheels and follow the coal truck" as it made deliveries, picking up the pieces as they fell off the truck. This was not considered stealing, but only another method of acquiring fuel. Collecting "wood from buildings in the process of being erected or torn down," however, could result in trouble. In 1909, "petty thievery of wood and coal" led the list of reasons for arrests of young boys in New York City.[50]

Some immigrant children, most often from Polish or Slovak families, lived in midwestern cities in small houses to which their parents, even though they were usually renters, not owners, devoted much time and attention. Rose Mary Prosen, from a Slovene family in Cleveland, reported that all her parents' free time was devoted to "painting . . . repairing the stairs, scrubbing, rubbing, scouring" or "planting a vegetable garden in their tiny front yard." For some immigrant families, home ownership was achieved early in the settlement process. Harriet Pawlowska, the daughter of a Polish immigrant bricklayer who settled in the expanding steel-making center of the United States, Detroit, grew up in a modest frame cottage with a front porch. Her father had bought the house with a borrowed $50 from a friend and spent $12 a month to pay off his $1,500 mortgage.[51]

In many respects, particularly housing, the children of migrant Hispanic farmworkers are more deprived than most other immigrant children in the United States today. In Florida, for example, they live in two-room crowded shacks with few conveniences. The National Coalition of Advocates for Students reported in 1985 that a father, mother, three children, and an infant shared a shack in which every room was filled with beds. Housing for the more permanent urban newcomers and their children varies greatly. Vietnamese shrimp fishermen in New Orleans live in shacks near the water that hold their means of making a living; Dominicans occupy the apartment houses in northern Manhattan that were once the homes of middle-class Jews; Central Americans live in small houses in New Jersey. Most are living in better quarters than their predecessors did at the same stage of settlement, but some are not.[52]

Many children of the latest immigrants, such as the Chinese who settled in New York City after the passage the Immigration Act of 1965, moved into housing that was not much better than that available 85 years earlier. A survey funded by the U.S. Department of Health, Education, and Welfare in 1977 found that most Chinatown apartments, inhabited by single male sojurners in the past, were rat and roach ridden, offered no privacy, and were much too small for the mothers and children who began to arrive when the new law made it possible for them to join fathers who had preceded them.

One family of six slept in an 8-by-10-foot room, another used three sets of bunk beds to provide sleeping quarters for two boys, two girls, and two parents. There was a bathroom in the latter apartment, but it was located in the much-used kitchen. Mrs. Chan, the mother, had hung a curtain around it, but as one of her daughters said, it could not take the place of a real bathroom.[53]

We do not know what this same daughter, now an adult, would say about the intangibles in her childhood home; immigrant children from groups that arrived earlier have memories of growing up with hardship and inconvenience but also recall their childhood homes as places of warmth and comfort. Marie Prisland, for example, recalled an iron stove that burned mostly wood and "crackled with a glowing warmth." In her Slovenian-American household the bread and cake of her homeland, baked in this oven, was eagerly received, and the baths given to the smallest children in a "washtub in front of the open door of the warm oven" were apparently great fun. Marie and her siblings especially loved the stove in winter, when "it warmed their cold and numb feet and dried their wet shoes and soggy mittens which were hung behind the stove." Prisland lived in Cleveland, but similar sentiments were part of the childhood memories of Harry Roskolenko, who grew up on the Lower East Side of Manhattan. "We had a real Russian Jewish home," he said, that included a three-tier bed (a delight when you are small), a Russian stove that warmed him and a samovar for tea.[54]

Warmth, both physical and emotional (Prisland remembers her "tight-knit" family seated around the beloved stove), may have been the stove's most valued function, but the meals prepared on it were surely as important, partly because the scarcity of food in their homeland was one of the reasons for their emigration. One Irish mother said that in her hometown people were always hungry and "often ate cress out of the brooks on oaten bread with a bit of lard." Conditions were only minimally better for Irish families who came to Boston, where, according to Oscar Handlin, many parents and children lived on the brink of starvation. This does not seem to be as typical for those who came to New York. Residents of the "Bloody Old Sixth" Ward were very poor, but Carol Groneman, who has chronicled their hardships, did not find as much desperation as Handlin found in Boston. In 1855, however, during one of the frequent downturns in the New York economy, they were in danger of starving.[55]

After their first grain crop was harvested, Norwegian immigrant children living on the praries usually ate an ample if monotonous diet of porridge and milk. They missed their fish and flatbread, but gradually grew accustomed to American food, especially beef and pork when it became available. As with most ethnic groups, holidays brought out traditional dishes and special desserts, which children fondly remembered. When a blizzard, drought, or grasshopper plague created abnormal problems, food was short. During one such moment, a Norwegian family was reduced to eating a very rough pudding, consisting of natural ingredients that the mother had gathered in the fields. When it was sufficiently baked, she set it in the cellar to cool. Her oldest daughter, a girl of eight, found it and, because she was starving, quickly ate it all. The result was tragic. Unable to digest so much roughage at one feeding, she died in agony.[56]

Other families, such as those where the breadwinner was an unskilled laborer and the children were numerous, economized wherever they could. To avoid spending money on milk, for example, Italian babies were weaned as late as possible. A Jewish mother managed her food supply differently. Faced with the need to satisfy the appetites of four growing sons on a small and irregular income, she cut the bread and cake she baked into the thinnest possible slices, ignoring the chorus of complaints from the boys who shouted, "Cut cake Mama, don't make splinters!"[57]

Partly because they were aware of the poverty in which many immigrant children lived and partly because they saw an opportunity to Americanize by exposing the immigrant youngsters to mainstream American food, the progressive reformers who were active at the turn of the century pressured urban schools to serve cheap nutritious lunches, which most of the immigrant children shunned. Observant Jewish children had a particular objection; the food served was not kosher. For most of the children, however, the problem was that it was unfamiliar. In any case, the immigrant youngsters voted with their feet. At lunchtime on the Lower East Side, for example, they took themselves and their pennies out of the building and, to the horror of their teachers, who saw spicy foods as a stimulant that could lead to alcoholism, spent their money on the kosher pickles sold on stands strategically located outside of the school building.[58] Many children went home for lunch, but if both parents worked or the distance between school and their apartment was too great, they remained near the school building. Recently arrived Italian families had no religious objections to school lunches, but regretted the loss of a long-standing custom that had united the family in their native land; having a large meal at noon with the entire family present. According to Pamatra Saran, a member of one of the Indian families who have arrived since 1965, they have a similar problem. Their children do not want to sit down at the table at all. Instead, they prefer American fast food, eaten on the run, to their mother's cooking.[59]

There are also some happy food stories, where children enjoyed eating the cuisine of their homeland with their parents. One Slovenian woman said that "no chicken today tastes like the chicken my mother prepared for Sunday dinner. There is no chicken soup today that tastes like the chicken soup my mother made from our home grown chickens." A Polish youngster recalls an entirely Polish diet, which caused her to value her ethnic identity more than she might otherwise have done. Her mother was a very good cook; especially before holidays, the smell of her cooking created joy and anticipation in her home.[60]

Practical reasons aside, food was of the greatest importance to immigrant children because they saw it as a symbol of love and caring that their overworked mothers often could not express any other way. It was solace when a child suffered injury in an often hostile environment; indeed, it provided strength to go out into that environment. At a time when most immigrant families could rarely buy toys or spare money for candy-store treats, home cooking was an expression of a mother's warmth. Even when they rebelled and wanted to eat "American style," their mother's food remained an important influence in most immigrant children's lives.

Health and Survival

Try as they might, however, the mothers in all ethnic groups could not always keep their children alive and well. Their task was difficult wherever they lived. A German immigrant mother living on a midwestern farm was devastated when her youngest son died of rheumatic fever following prolonged exposure to cold. "My Peter is gone. I walk my house alone. A part of me is gone when my small Peter goes from me." The cold was an enemy in the prairie states. A son of Norwegian immigrants living in Minnesota recalled wearing "two suits of long underwear, two flannel shirts, two pair of pants, a vest, a heavy coat and two or three pairs of mittens" when he helped with the chores.[61] Sometimes all the clothing in the house could not prevent illness and death because neither a doctor nor medicine was available. The same Norwegian boy who remembered his winter wardrobe so vividly also saw his two little sisters die of diphtheria, which his mother's home remedies could not cure. A Danish mother in Iowa suffered even greater pain when she failed to understand an itinerant peddler's instructions on how to treat her daughter's lung and throat ailment and administered the skunk oil he had sold her internally instead of just rubbing it on. Again, extremely cold weather had created a problem and lack of adequate medical care had led to a death.[62]

Many other ailments afflicted farm children, immigrants and otherwise. Some diseases, such as whooping cough, scarlet fever, and measles, were also part of growing up in the city, but others were specific to farm life. Written recollections describe "festering sores on small feet," the result of running "barefooted on the burnt over prairie, chilblains from exposure to glacial cold, sunstroke from field labor, puncture wounds from stray pitchforks, bruises and broken bones from livestock hooves." Cholera deaths were not limited to cities; Norwegian settlements in the upper Mississippi valley suffered through epidemics several times in the 1840s and 1850s.[63]

High rates of infant and child injury were not limited to farm families. Urban Irish children with foreign-born parents died in greater numbers than children of the native-born. One out of four infants born to Irish immigrant mothers in New York died in infancy, and even if they lived, they had only a limited chance to survive past their fifth birthday. Robert Ernst, writing about those who lived in New York in 1855, says that "the Irish were the chief victims of whatever contagious diseases appeared in the city." The same could be said of the Irish who settled in the Massachusetts milltown of Lawrence, where 40–45 percent of the deaths of children under three years old were from immigrant families.[64]

A "filthy environment made child survival hazardous and in a society where children were numerous and mothers had to work to support them, neglect was the natural result." In Boston, for example, there was a rise in infant mortality after 1845, attributed to overcrowding and inefficient drainage in the poorer districts. In 1849, 500 of the 700 people that died during a cholera epidemic in that city were Irish men, women, and children. Infant mortality among the Irish who lived in slum districts was high, but the remarkable fecundity of the women replaced those who were lost, assuring large families well into the second generation. Handlin said the the Irish "repopulated" Boston, filling the gap left by the low birth rate of WASP women.[65]

Good health and survival were not much more assured for immigrant children who arrived later in the nineteenth century, and perhaps as a result birth rates continued to be high. Polish and Slavic parents in the Midwest, for example, did not restrict the the size of their family because they wanted to be sure that at least one child would be around to care for them in their old age. In 1900, one third of Italian and Polish women in Pittsburgh saw their children die in their first year of life. Dr. Antonio Stella, who treated Italian children in Little Italy and East Harlem in New York City, saw many cases of tuberculosis. Several articles in *Charities* magazine showed how the alley housing in the Italian districts of Philadelphia led to the spread of this disease.[66] A Jewish woman who had been a young mother in 1906 recalled her terror when, during a hot Philadelphia summer, her first-born baby daughter contracted the dreaded infant diarrhea and all that her doctor could prescribe was fresh air. Since she lived in back of a tiny candy store that had almost no air, she sat on the curb with her baby day and night until the weather cooled and the child was able to retain food and liquid and so end the dehydration that had threatened her life.[67]

Poverty, more than any other factor, explains the high mortality rate among the Italian immigrants who arrived in the same period. In Buffalo, New York, for example, Italian families with higher incomes had more surviving children; poorer families were smaller owing to higher death rates. Indeed, Virginia Yans-McLaughlin, who has studied the community closely, suggests that child mortality was a form of birth control. "In 1900," she writes, "60 to 89 percent of Italian women over 30 years had at least one child die." In larger terms, only 600 of every 1,000 Italian infants survived, and the figure for Polish babies in Buffalo was similar. Some, because of improper care by poorly trained midwives, never made it through the birth process; others died from cholera, tuberculosis, and other illnesses contracted in their dirty and unsanitary homes.[68]

Sometimes, even the formalities of a child's death were unmanageable. A Polish single mother, herself suffering from tuberculosis, had to go to the United Charities of Chicago for help with funeral expenses for her baby, sickly from birth and now dead. The infant had been born out of wedlock, and so her church would not help her; the father, a temporary boarder in her home, disappeared, and she had five other children. In the end, her brother bought a gravesite, and she raised enough from friends and neighbors to bury the child.[69]

This poor woman was something of an exception. Illegitimate children were born to many immigrant women, but Poles were not high on the list drawn by Nils Carpenter for the U.S. Department of Commerce in 1920. Indeed, his figures showed that American-born white women were most likely to bear children out of wedlock. Immigrants from the British Isles and Scandinavia topped his foreign-born list; among the newer immigrants, Italians and Jews were at the bottom and Slavic women in the middle.[70]

Illegitimate children were often orphans. The father, if known, usually did not remain nearby, and the mother, left without a means of support, had to turn her children over to an institution. Immigrant children, illegitimate or not, were also often orphaned by parental death. Widows or widowers might literally work themselves to death to support their children, and it was not unusual for both parents to die when their children were quite young. Sometimes there was enough of an extended family to take charge, but many parents had left their relatives behind. As a result, thousands of children, many from immigrant families, lived on the streets and were arrested for vagrancy in Boston, New York, Philadelphia, and Baltimore.

Few in the Irish or German communities in Boston and New York were able to make large contributions to charitable institutions. Native-born "do-gooders" took over the task of sheltering homeless children. In New York, Protestants established the Childrens Aid Society (CAS). To keep Catholic children out of CAS institutions, Archbishop John Hughes organized his own Society for the Protection of Destitute Catholic Children in the City of New York, with the aim of rehabilitating delinquent and neglected children, especially Irish ones. He also brought over additional Sisters of Charity to staff the new institutions. When even more space was needed, Hughes followed the example of the CAS and placed homeless children in apprentice programs (which offered room and board as well as the chance to learn a trade) whenever he could. They were also placed in foster homes and, borrowing another practice from the CAS, sent to Catholic families in the West.[71]

With some exceptions, such as the children of Mexican migrant workers who have a very high infant mortality rate and suffer from malnutrition, anemia, and tuberculosis, immigrant children who have come to the United States since 1965, regardless of ethnicity or where they settle, have a much greater chance of survival because medical knowledge has progressed and health care is more widely available. In most places, children cannot be enrolled in school without proof of immunization, although, as one Hmong boy in La Playa, California, said, the "shots" were worse than going to school, which he also did not like very much. One group of Asian immigrants, Koreans, have small families, but the reason is lower fertility, not high child mortality. Chinese families are also smaller than those of earlier immigrant groups, but again not because the children die young. In spite of the congested and poor-quality housing in New York's Chinatown, child mortality figures are no higher than those for the city as a whole.[72]

Nativism

To a greater or lesser degree, all the immigrant groups who chose to settle in the United States were victims of nativism and bigotry. While adults felt the impact most directly because of employment and housing discrimination, their children, at school, work, or play, were also affected. In Lawrence,

Massachusetts, where in the middle of the nineteenth century Irish immigrants and their children, as we have seen, faced poor housing, disease and early death, they also experienced virulent anti-Catholicism. Donald Cole, who has chronicled their suffering, says that Lawrence was well known for its bigotry, but the same could be said for other places in which Irish immigrants settled. It was certainly the case near Boston, where a convent school in neighboring Charlestown was "torched" in 1834. In Boston proper, many help-wanted advertisements said, "None need apply but Americans."[73]

In New York employers blamed the Irish for creating labor unrest, and native-born workers accused them of lowering wages. The second charge was heard more often. A short-lived New York City newspaper, *Champion of American Labor,* wanted to stop the "swarms of . . . paupers from European poorhouses" from entering the city and taking their jobs. Such sentiments were widespread. Three years earlier, the candidate of an overtly nativist group known as the Order of the Star Spangled Banner, whose members were referred to as "Know Nothings," was elected mayor. As more and more impoverished Irish immigrants entered the city, nativist arguments centered on the money spent on their support as well as on the crimes they committed, the filthy conditions of their neighborhood, and their propensity to riot. These charges were echoed in Boston, where the Irish lived "on the brink of starvation, even when at work," and needed charity when discarded by an overstocked labor market.[74]

Only very young children could be unaware of the hostility exhibited by the outside world. As they grew older, they learned about nativism from the stories of their parents and older siblings; when they went out into the world, they experienced bigotry themselves. Advertisements and real estate notices made it clear that many parts of the city and many occupations were closed to Irish immigrants. Some of the hostility they experienced was diluted by the Church, which grew more important as the number of Catholics in the port cities increased. Parochial schools also shielded Irish boys and girls from some of the nativism.

German children, arriving in the United States at about the same time as the Irish, do not seem to have had serious problems with bigotry. They were given pejorative nicknames, and their parents' desire to maintain the continental Sunday, complete with beer halls, brought criticism, but on the whole even German Catholics were accepted where the Irish were not. One reason for this was that as a group Germans were less likely to require financial assistance. Another was that, unlike the Irish, they did not gravitate only to the port cities but could be found, in greater or lesser numbers, in every state in the Union. They were most numerous in the Midwest, and in those states they not only escaped overt nativism but were able to use their political clout to achieve their own goals. In Wisconsin and Illinois, for example, they defeated legislators who had voted for laws requiring that all children receive part of their education in English. As a result, those laws were repealed and their children learned the German language and culture, taught by German teachers in tax-supported public schools.[75]

Unfortunately, the discrimination and rejection suffered by Irish young-sters did not make them tolerant of other groups. As a result, they were the Gentiles most feared by Jewish children, who formed gangs of their own, partly to prevent injury at the hands of the dreaded "Irishers" but also for other reasons. Jewish gangs, half social and half delinquent, had been formed as early as the 1880s but became more visible after the turn of the century. By 1902, there were more than 300 Jewish boys in various reformatories in New York, and five years later the problem was important enough to warrant the construction of the Hawthorne School, a reformatory in Westchester County supported by the German Jewish community. Most of the crimes committed by the inmates involved thievery; "grifters" hung out wherever the crowds were large enough to make pickpocketing worthwhile.[76]

Gang violence was one way of coping with bigotry; avoidance was another. Jewish parents in New York, when presented with an opportunity to move their children from a crowded school on the Lower East Side to an underutilized school on the Irish West Side, refused, on grounds of safety, to do so. All Hallow's Eve was a particularly dangerous time. One Jewish girl who lived in Brooklyn in the 1920s was forbidden to leave the house on that day because Irish gangs roamed the streets with a distinctive weapon, one of their mother's long black stockings filled with stones, which when swung built up momentum and could cause serious injury.[77]

Given the hostility, it comes as no surprise to learn that elderly Jews who were children between 1900 and 1914, although they had lived in solidly Jewish enclaves, had not forgotten how much they feared the Catholics who lived in nearby neighborhoods. For those who lived in areas where they were in the minority, the problems were even greater. In the first place, they were often living there because their parents owned a shop of some kind. Although their family might have no more money than their working-class neighbors, this placed them at a somewhat higher social level and earned them envy and dislike. Until Vatican II, Catholic children were taught that Jews were responsible for the death of Christ. As a result, the streets frequently echoed with cries of "Christ-Killer," accompanied by physical action to match. Some of the hostility was based on lack of infor-mation. Other than street contact, Irish and Jewish children did not know each other. They attended different schools, celebrated different holy days, and heard different messages at home.[78]

Jewish storekeepers found it difficult to move away from their cus-tomers, but those not so attached attempted to leave areas like the Lower East Side or similar sections of Brooklyn as soon as their income permitted. In most cases they were able to follow in the footsteps of previous occupants of Lower Manhattan, who had fled the "invasion" of Jews and Italians and settled in better housing in Upper Manhattan, the Bronx, and Brooklyn.

By the 1920s some Jews were financially able to purchase small houses in Queens and Brooklyn, but at that point the process of ethnic succession broke down. Real estate advertisements discouraged them from looking for housing in Jackson Heights, Queens, or Flatbush in Brooklyn by saying "restrictions" or "sensibly priced, sensibly built, sensibly restricted." Fortunately, although restrictions were unpleasant, middle-class Jewish children were not forced to remain in the slums. Their parents found other, equally pleasant areas developed by Jewish builders, where they were welcome and could live among their own.[79]

Much more painful was the prospect of facing employment and educational discrimination when they grew up. But as with housing, the sons and daughters of the Jewish immigrants who had arrived before World War I understood that certain occupations, such as white-collar work in large insurance companies, and the professions, such as medicine or engineering, were usually beyond their reach. As the Irish had done earlier by entering politics and thus acquiring government jobs, Jews accommodated themselves by starting small businesses, becoming service personnel in larger Jewish-owned businesses, or going abroad to attend medical school.[80]

Other immigrant children were not exempt from the bigotry directed at Jews. An investigation of 734 Italian children, aged 11–15 in five New York City public schools, revealed that they were very much aware of where they stood with their teachers and non-Italian peers. The former saw them as poor students and the latter as unsuitable friends. This was also true for other immigrant youngsters. Classmates told a young girl from a Slovak family in Ohio that she "talked funny," and a Portuguese boy in Cambridge, Massachusetts, was often "picked on" by his American peers. On one occasion, severely provoked, he took his grandfather's knife and used it in a fight. As a result, he was badly hurt in a subsequent fracas with the injured boy's friends. There must have been thousands of such incidents, some even more serious, but even a child who shunned violence was affected, emotionally, if not physically, by bigotry.[81]

Some, however, spent at least part of their childhood without feeling unwanted. A boy who was born into an immigrant home in heavily Polish South Chicago was unaware of the fact that Poles were held in low esteem until he attended a Catholic preparatory school outside of the enclave in which he had grown up. "It was here that I first encountered people . . . who saw in my Polish identity reason to hold me in contempt." His experience is instructive. For many immigrant children, their family and the ethnic enclave in which they lived protected them from the worst effects of bigotry until they emerged into the larger world of high school, college, professional school, or the job market.[82]

There were very few Chinese or Japanese children in the United States before the 1880s, but those that were here experienced extreme racism. The

San Francisco Board of Education used an 1872 state law that required separate schools for children of "Mongolian descent" to set up a Chinese school. When Japanese children began to arrive later in the nineteenth century, they attended white schools until their numbers grew larger and brought protests from white parents "complaining of the enforced association of their children with Japanese immigrants." Nothing was done until after the earthquake in 1906, when pressure from labor unions and other nativists led the school board to take action. The Chinese School was renamed the Oriental School, and the 93 Japanese children were barred from other schools and forced to attend. As is well known, angry protests from the Japanese government led President Theodore Roosevelt to intervene. The Oriental School remained, but it was not the only school in San Francisco that Japanese children could attend.[83]

Growing up in the mining town of Washington, California, one Chinese woman remembered that the white children "were not nice to us at all. They yelled 'Ching, Chong Chinamen sitting on a rail' when they saw us approach the school. We hated it but didn't answer back because there were so many more of them than us." A young Chinese boy handled a similar problem in a different way. When a white student who needed to know how to work out an arithmetic problem approached him and said, "Hey Chink, how do you do this?" he "let him have it." When the study hall teacher asked him what had happened, the boy said, "I was showing him the Chinky way to solve a problem."[84]

What has been the experience of the children of the newest immigration? Passage of laws regarding refugees and the revision of other immigration regulations such as those that deal with undocumented aliens has resulted in the entry of many new groups of immigrant children. In 1989, for example, in a Queens elementary school, English was a foreign tongue to half the students, who among them spoke thirty languages, including Spanish, Chinese, Haitian, Creole, and Korean. Three years later, 65,322 students who were born in a foreign country entered the New York City public schools. In other parts of the United States, such as the West Coast, Japanese and the languages of Southeast Asia, such as Hmong, are heard in the school hallways and playgrounds every day.[85]

For many of these children, the process of adjustment is eased by bilingual programs, but this does not shield them from bigotry. Haitian youngsters suffer hostility from their black American peers as well as from Spanish-speaking youngsters from other parts of the Caribbean, who call them "Frenchies" and beat them up. One teacher in a New York City school kept her Haitian students in school for an extra 15 minutes "in the hope that their Hispanic peers would go home rather than wait to pounce upon the Haitians." These same Hispanic youngsters are often victims themselves, frequently at the hands of native-born blacks. Predictably, they have formed gangs, and, as was true for the Jews, Irish, and Italians in the past, the gangs have criminal purposes as well as defensive ones.[86]

English-speaking immigrant children from the British West Indies are distinguished from other blacks by their speech, but as Selina, a young member of a family that emigrated from Barbados and settled in Brooklyn, discovered, a stellar performance in a school dance festival did not prevent humiliation at the party that followed. The white hostess, her friends's mother, questioned her closely, and when she found out that Selina's roots were in the West Indies, told her how much she had liked a West Indian houseworker she had employed because "she left the house spotless." After more of this, the woman asked Selina to "say something in that delightful West Indian accent for us," at which point Selina bolted and ran through the streets, filled with hatred and self-hatred.[87]

The children of other groups who are part of the new era of immigration that began in 1965 have not been spared the bigotry that was the pattern of the past. In spite of changes, legal and attitudinal, prejudice and nativism are still present in American society, reflected by what children say and do to those who are unfamiliar to them. Soviet Jewish youngsters in Brooklyn, for example, complain that they are shunned by their American peers and often have to defend themselves against classmates who resent their presence. Mexican children in the Southwest are called "beaners" and are said to eat out of garbage cans. When a 10-year-old Vietnamese girl was asked if she had experienced racism, she said, diplomatically, "Well, it would be better to be white." Other Asians, particularly Koreans, are subjected to considerable hostility, especially in black communities.[88]

Chinese children, partly because they are so numerous in certain neighborhoods and therefore in the majority in the schools they attend and partly because they are seen as a "model minority" by their teachers, are less likely to be victims of overt bigotry. In New York's Chinatown, for example, they attend de facto segregated elementary and middle schools and comprise a large part of the student body at nearby Seward Park High School. In other areas of the city, however, they are sometimes victimized by the "dark kids," mainly Hispanic, with whom they share the schools. This, however, is not the pattern in most of the districts into which middle-class Chinese have moved. Children from families living in Queens neighborhoods such as Jackson Heights and Flushing are only one group in this most polyglot section of the city, and perhaps because almost everyone in their classes has come from somewhere else, it is difficult to be a nativist.[89]

None of the recent young arrivals from the Far East, however, have suffered as Japanese children did between 1941 and 1943, when as a result of U.S. government policy, 50,000 of them were removed, with their parents, from West Coast areas and interned farther inland. Because immigration laws had blocked the entry of most Japanese women between 1908 and 1924, a majority of the Nisei (American-born Japanese) were at most teenagers when U.S. participation in World War II began.

At first, the Japanese families were moved from their homes to temporary and uncomfortable holding camps to await the completion of more permanent housing at various places in the Southwest. Parents and children had many problems in the camps, most notably a lack of privacy. One family's quarters were separated from another's by thin partitions, which led one father of an 18-month-old boy to say, "The worst part was not to be able to bring up the baby right. If you were living in your own house, you could let him cry but here you have got to shut him up in some way because you could not let him bother the people on the other side of the partition."[90]

For other parents, it was the public meals that distressed them most. A mother and her young daughter, for example, had to eat at a table with two undisciplined little boys who caused havoc during mealtimes. In a number of ways, the internment experience was particularly harmful for parents and their children. For one thing, parental authority was greatly diminished, weakened by their inability to do anything to prevent the internment and replaced by the orders of the authorities who administered the camps. For another, as the months went on, young and middle-aged Japanese who did not have children were able to leave the camps for service on farms or in the military, leaving behind the oldest, the youngest, and those needed to take care of them. For teenagers, however, the experience was not all bad. In contrast to their position in public schools before the war, "in the camps they became student body leaders, captains of athletic teams and editors of yearbooks."[91] But this was only a temporary change. Even when World War II ended and Japanese families were free to settle where they wished, bigotry remained a problem for the children. White American children would lump all Asian children together and chant "Chink, Chink, Chink" when they could get away with it. As late as 1975, the Sansei (third-generation Japanese) felt uncomfortable with Caucasians who still categorized them as foreigners.[92]

Mexicans are another immigrant group that has long been the target of bigotry. Anglo hostility in the Southwest and California continue to cause much pain to immigrant Mexican children. In a segment from *Chicano Poems from the Barrio,* Angelo de Hoyas says:

This land belongs to a pilgrim
arrived here only yesterday
whose racist tongue says to me:
I hate Meskins. You're a Meskin.
Why don't you go back where you came from?[93]

Given the fact that Mexicans preceded Anglos in the southwestern United States by several centuries, the question is ridiculous. It is not, however, a question that has been asked only of Mexicans.

In various accents, in various places, and at all times, the children of immigrants have been asked this question, and the resulting feeling of not being wanted has been perhaps the most important factor distinguishing their lives from those whose families have been in American for generations. Some aspects of the immigrant child's experience, such as poverty, poor housing, loss of parents, and ill health are hazards many children must face, but other factors are unique to those born elsewhere and brought to the United States or born to immigrant parents after arrival. The trauma of resettlement, including the need to learn a new language and new ways, most difficult for those taken from their birthplace as preadolescents, was something most American-born children did not have to face. For many reasons, the children of the "uprooted" had an abbreviated childhood. A difficult journey on land and sea, an uncertain welcome, and the struggle to survive in an unfamiliar and often hostile environment have shaped the world of immigrant children, as have the greater opportunities for a better life available to many of them.

2

In the Classroom

From the beginning of mass immigration in the 1840s to the present day, the majority of Americans, whether they welcomed immigrants or not, believed that it was essential to educate the foreign-born as well as the native-born. There were several reasons for this. Immigrant homes and neighborhoods were neither peaceful nor safe, and "educators believed that children living amidst disorder required some semblance of order in their lives if they were to grow up into responsible adults."[1] Public schools, therefore, emphasized routine and discipline above all else. Wherever possible, this kind of training began early. Beginning in St. Louis in 1873, public kindergartens, intended "to remove immigrant slum children from the city streets where they were clearly learning wrong ideas and habits," began to appear in many American cities receiving immigrants. The five year olds who were enrolled were taught "habits of regularity, punctuality, silence, obedience and self control."[2]

Next in importance was Americanization. If the schools failed to turn the "little aliens" into "little citizens," the "balkanization of America" would follow. Successful Americanization via the public schools, on the other hand, would create a unified, strong nation. In the middle of the nineteenth century, it was generally agreed that the purpose of education was assimilation. During the period of heaviest immigration, 1880–1914, therefore, Americanization was the goal. Most members of the established society saw no place for cultural diversity. The immigrants themselves often thought otherwise. In Cincinnati, Louisville, Indianapolis, St. Louis, and St. Paul, Germans defeated attempts to make public schools "German-free," and, as we shall see, other groups wanted more than an American education for their children.[3] Poles, Jews, and Chinese, like the Germans, wanted their children to go to ethnic schools so they could understand the language and customs of their parents, but when faced with the cost and the opposition of their children, they settled for after-school classes in Hebrew, Polish, and Chinese, to name the most common.

What can be stated with absolute certainty, however, is that the matter of educating immigrant children was and is a political "hot potato." Diane Ravitch discusses three major educational wars fought in New York City: in the 1840s, when Irish immigrants wanted public funds to operate their parochial schools; in the 1890s, when WASP reformers campaigned for a centralized school system to Americanize Italians and Jews; and, most recently, in the 1960s, when blacks and Hispanics fought to control their inadequate, de facto segregated neighborhood schools. In each case the battle was really about power, clothed in an educational guise. The first school war, in 1842, matched Archbishop John Hughes against a Protestant-dominated, publicly funded charitable organization, the Public School Society. The second war, roughly 50 years later, pitted the Tammany political machine against the good-government forces of the Public Education Association. In 1968, the issue was centralized versus decentralized schools or, to put it baldly, who was going to have control over funds allocated to the public schools.[4]

At this moment, in the last decade of the twentieth century, increased immigration and a revival of ethnic nationalism have renewed the battle. The virtues and disadvantages of bilingualism, multiculturalism, and English as a Second Language (ESL) are passionately discussed by educators and laypeople alike. The city on the Hudson River has been a bellwether for the study of ethnic diversity, but much of what has happened there has been thoroughly explored elsewhere. This chapter will focus less on the various battles over education policy and more on the young scholars and their families: parental attitudes (young children, after all, do not make basic educational decisions), children's reactions to their school experiences, and, finally, the extent to which the children of the foreign-born have used the educational opportunities available to them.

Attitudes

German and Irish families were, in general, not opposed to a primary school education for their children and were also in agreement on the dangers inherent in public school education. Their reasons, however, differed. For the former, it was largely a cultural matter; for the latter a matter of faith and morals. Some Irish parents attacked the public schools for excluding religious education and, at least in Protestant Boston, considered compulsory education in such schools "kidnapping." Secular teachers would weaken a child's ties to parents, they said, and lead to "disobedience, smoking, drinking and blasphemous talk about fornication." Unfortunately, in light of their strong views on public schools, Catholic parents in Boston and New York, where they were most numerous, were too poor to maintain as many parochial schools as were needed.[5]

In 1840, Archbishop John Hughes, the leader of the New York community, estimated "that Catholic institutions could absorb only 4,000 to 5,000 of the 9,000 to 12,000 Catholic children of the city," and it was for this reason that he led the battle against the Public School Society, which operated secular schools maintained by taxpayer money but governed by a private board of trustees. Sometimes, as in Boston, Irish Catholic insistence on parochial education became a shield for truancy.[6]

Education was not compulsory in either city when German and Irish youngsters began to arrive in large numbers, but even if it had been the law, it would not have made much difference. Most mid-nineteenth-century immigrant parents did not associate schooling with upward mobility and did not see their accustomed way of life as needing revision, something that the school authorities appeared to believe was necessary. In New York, young German children who could not be squeezed into the *Freie Deutsche Schule* used two of the society's schools, which offered a one-year bilingual program. Older children of both groups attended no school at all. Religious and cultural reasons aside, many immigrant families were too poor to send their 10 year olds to any school and instead, as we shall see in chapter 3, sent them to work at an early age.[7]

Irish and German Catholics were not in a position to build a strong parochial school system until they had established an adequate economic base and were able to support enough of the kind of schools they wanted. German Protestants had more success because their cultural desires did not raise issues of church and state. Their language and history could be incorporated into the standard public school curriculum, whereas Catholic theology could not. They certainly faced opposition, but in communities where Germans could muster sufficient political strength, their children were taught the language and culture of their homeland. German Jews, who made up a substantial part of the German community, did not object to their fellow Germans' eagerness to preserve Old World culture, partly because they also valued that culture but also because they did not see schooling beyond basic literacy as terribly important. Immigrant Jews from the various German states were more interested in having their sons learning business or a trade through apprenticeships. Marriage was their goal for a daughter.[8]

Interestingly, although they represented a significant portion of the population of Minnesota and neighboring states in the 1880s, Swedish immigrant parents accepted the fact that in the United States, "children never received any Christian education in the public schools." Parents, they believed, must take care of religious matters themselves. A mother who explained this in a letter to her relatives in Sweden went on to say that when her children had "learned everything they are to learn in English," she and her husband would send them to a Swedish-speaking Lutheran pastor for confirmation instruction.[9]

The attitudes of immigrants from Northern and Western Europe toward schooling were more clear cut than the positions taken by the Italians, Jews, Slavs, and Poles who came after them. The traditional view is that Jews were eager to have their children attend public school and that the children from the other groups that came in the late nineteenth and early twentieth centuries were not. Both of these positions, however, require modification. Although the accepted view continues to see first-, second-, and possibly even later-generation Italian youngsters as reluctant scholars, in recent years the reasons for these attitudes have been more carefully explored, leading to the conclusion that Italians' hostility to schooling, given their history and condition in urban America, was entirely rational.

From several sources, it appears that training a child to be attuned to the family's welfare was the educational aim of most Italian immigrant parents. Richard Varbero, writing about Italians in South Philadelphia, said that although Italian working-class parents were aware that formal education could lead a son to become a *dottore* or *avvocato,* they "subordinated unrealistic social aspirations to immediate economic gain." Richard Ulin's 1975 book, based on interviews with Italian American children in Winchester, Massachusetts, conducted in the late 1950s, revealed that the offspring of Italian parents were equally negative about the value of education. They told Ulin that influence and charm were more important than schooling in getting ahead, and their underrepresentation in the local high school proved the point.[10]

Other scholars have said that Italian parents saw little use for schools, indeed actively resented some school activities. One mother, exasperated when her son stayed for sports after school, slapped him on the head and told him to "quit playing and go to work." Many immigrants from southern Italy wanted their sons to leave school early and get on-the-job training. Several authors say that Italian mothers and fathers saw the public school as hostile to their values and resented the teacher's attempts to impart information that was, in their view, of no value to their children's lives. A Sicilian father in Providence, Rhode Island, said, "what a boy learns is what his father and mother think is best for him." Some Italian parents apparently accepted the adage, "Don't make your children better than you are."[11]

In spite of much evidence to the contrary, some historians have maintained that as a group Italians were not opposed to education. Their work has been criticized and has not changed the traditional view, but their efforts have instigated closer examination. In Providence, for example, it appears that Italian parents did want their sons to get better jobs but believed that apprenticeship, not vocational education, was the way to achieve this. A study done in Newark, New Jersey, in 1942 indicated that a number of Italian parents did see the connection between education and good jobs, but for a variety of reasons were unable to keep their sons in school for any length of time.[12]

As was true for the Irish who had come before the Italians, poverty often meant that the mother of a family had to go to work if a child was to go to school, something distasteful to most Italian husbands. Furthermore, for those who disliked America and planned to return to Italy as soon as they had enough money to buy land there, it seemed foolish to have a child give up earnings to learn a language he would never need. As it turned out, their assumption proved to be mistaken. Most Italian families remained in the United States partly because their children refused to go back. Whether they hoped to buy property in Italy or in America, however, the money their children earned would bring about the desired purchase sooner.

Longing for land of their own stemmed from centuries of exploitation in southern Italy and Sicily. Other attitudes that impeded the attainment of education by Italians were also the result of experiences in their homeland. There was, for example, no reason for them to respect intellectuals or want their children to emulate them because they had been shunned by the Italian intelligentsia for generations. Ideas like this boded ill for their children's success in American schools. Schoolmaster Leonard Covello, in his classic book on the Italian American child, connects the immigrant background and the American school experience more thoroughly than anyone else. Because the schools in the Old Country were "controlled from and based on norms applicable to North Italy," the "contadini" of southern Italy hated them. Indeed, he thought that the "burdensome imposition of Italian school laws" and fees were an incentive to emigrate. Gary Mormino, a student of Italian immigrants in St. Louis, shed additional light on their educational background. He found that in Lombardy girls aged 5–12 worked in the mills and that the rare child who did go to school left at age 11.[13]

If Covello is correct, Italian immigrant parents must have been sorely disappointed when they came to Boston, New York, Chicago, or Philadelphia, where the compulsory education laws were in direct conflict with their belief that children must contribute to family income. As one immigrant father told Mormino in St. Louis, "a family's wealth depends on the number of hands it has." Furthermore, what the child was being taught when he or she could have been working was interfering "with the patterns of family life."

This was particularly true for girls, who were expected to work and marry young and therefore would have no use for any idea the public school might plant in their heads. One Italian mother who opposed schooling for her daughter said the girl did not need to be literate because all she would do with her knowledge was write to her boyfriends. On the whole, Italian immigrant parents saw formal education beyond the statutory age as being appropriate only for the *prominenti*. For all these reasons, immigrant and first-generation Italian immigrant children spent as little time as possible in school.[14]

Although they did not settle in the same geographical areas and their number was smaller, immigrants from Central Europe, such as Slavs and Poles, held similar attitudes. In general, they resented and resisted the schools' attempts to transform their children into "unhyphenated" Americans and demonstrated their opposition by establishing parochial and folk schools wherever they could afford to do so. Although religious factors loomed larger for Poles, they were particularly hostile to public schools for historical reasons similar to those of the Italians. As had been true for the latter, formal education had been imposed on their children by outsiders. Without political power, Poles had been unable to prevent forced education in Russified schools and were determined not to be put in the same position in the United States.

Unlike the Italians, however, they were able to establish parochial schools to accommodate their children. Their reasons were quite clear: they feared that in public schools their children would lose their religious faith and become alienated from their culture. The parochial schools allowed the early Polish immigrants to preserve their language and history, something Bohemians were also eager to do, but when they petitioned the Chicago school board to allow such instruction in schools where more than half of the children were Bohemian, permission was refused. Unlike the Germans who preceded them, this much smaller community did not have the political clout to get its way.[15]

First- and second-generation Poles, wherever they went to school, usually ended their education at or immediately after the sixth grade. Like the Italians, they did not see the connection between formal schooling and upward mobility until the 1950s, when they accepted the idea that their children's lives should be "significantly different from their own." A machinist father in North Dakota, for example, speaking to his children in the 1950s, told them to study hard, go to college, get a white-collar job, and not "come home all smelly and dirty like me." Such an attitude had been accepted by some Central European immigrants a generation earlier. Ewa Morawska's study of the Johnstown, Pennsylvania, community of Central Europeans indicates that parental approval of schooling for upward mobility appeared during the 1920s.[16]

As was true for Slavic immigrants in other cities and for the Italians discussed earlier, the money a child could earn was, in many cases, essential. Uncompensated industrial accidents, illness, and sporadic unemployment all required that income be earned by a child when the customary breadwinner could not work. Even when there was no emergency, however, additional money was welcome, either to keep in reserve for bad times or to save for home ownership. "Slowly and painstakingly, immigrant families accumulated the capital needed for a first mortgage payment on a house." There were also some other reasons for sending children to work, not school, such as pocketing the money they earned and sending it to "relatives in the old country as a present for Christmas or to purchase an additional cow." In general, the children agreed that family came first and willingly left school for work.[17]

One Central European group of immigrants held a different attitude toward formal education. Joseph Barton's study of Romanians who settled in Cleveland indicated that the immigrant fathers in this community did see schooling as an effective path to upward mobility. More than 90 percent of the youngsters in his sample of second-generation Romanian sons in Cleveland, for example, finished high school, and 70 percent went to college or received a professional education. One reason for this, Barton thinks, was that Romanians had smaller families than Italians or Slovaks and were less interested in parochial schools. Going to public school, he suggests, offered social advantages denied to Polish children in parochial schools attended solely by youngsters from Catholic working-class families. This may be true. Certainly, in a public school, the young Romanians would be exposed to the generally more positive educational attitudes of the Jewish youngsters who would be their classmates.[18]

As a group, Russian and Polish Jewish parents favored formal education for their children to a greater extent than other immigrant groups, and therefore their sons and, to a lesser extent, their daughters were enrolled in the public schools of all the cities in which they settled. The qualifier "as a group," however, is important. Regardless of the respect religious Jews held for their learned men and of the fact that more of the males were literate than was true for other immigrants, the poverty they faced upon arrival and often for many years thereafter prevented the first- and second-generation of Jewish immigrant children from using formal education as extensively as is usually assumed.

Would they have kept their sons in school longer if they could have done without the income they could earn? Probably. In general, they approved of public schools and were ready to accept (indeed, often welcomed) the de facto segregation in the urban neighborhood schools their children attended. They did not protest when time for religious study was denied, when children were penalized for absences on important holy days or were forced to attend assembly programs that included New Testament readings and Christian hymns. Those who cared and could afford it sent their sons for after-school Hebrew lessons or to a "folkschule" and continued to use the free public schools for basic education.[19]

In spite of a generally favorable attitude at home, however, many Jewish children did not like school and did not do well. Truancy and a tendency to drop out early were problems in heavily Jewish schools, although not quite as severe as in those areas in which Italians predominated. Also, there were Jewish dullards as well as able students; some Lower East Side New York youngsters "went to school dancing" while others dragged their heels. The monolithic picture of Jewish school success, like most monoliths, must be adjusted for reality. A combination of economic need, distaste for learning, and other opportunities led first- and second-generation Jews into entrepreneurship (usually petty, such as peddling), not the halls of academe.[20]

Parents and children from the groups that have been arriving in the United States since 1965 to a certain extent echo the attitudes toward formal education of those who preceded them. There are also marked differences. Some, such as the Mexicans, are continuing a pattern of migration and settlement begun many years earlier; others, such as the Dominicans, are truly newcomers. There have been Asian children in American schools for most of the twentieth century, but they occupy a much more prominent position today. Similarly, Russian Jewish immigration, as we have seen, is nothing new, but those now coming from Eastern Europe are quite different from those who arrived before World War I.

How do the new arrivals see American public schools? Mexicans are generally grouped with the older immigrants, such as Italians, who did not see "the long range benefits that might accrue to their children from a good education." As was also true for some of the Italians, some Mexicans see themselves as temporary residents. In the past, their opposition to schooling was understandable. Even if Mexican parents intended to stay, the schools were not prepared to educate their children.[21]

This is not as true today, but in spite of greater understanding and ESL classes, Mexican parents do not urge school attendance beyond the primary grades for their sons and expect even less for their daughters. The memoir of a Mexican American girl describes her struggle to complete high school and use a college scholarship in the face of adamant opposition from her father, who arranged a marriage for her when she was 15. He was a poor migrant worker who could not accept his daughter's view that "if I were to escape from the migrant life I was going to have to master English." With her mother's help, she was allowed to attend high school for two years while also working in the fields, but after that she had to wage an even more bitter and divisive battle for further schooling.[22]

Another group of new arrivals, the Portuguese, are also expanding an older settlement and, like the Mexicans, are lukewarm about schools. As a group, they have a low literacy rate and retain the traditional view that children should consider family goals over their own and go to work as soon as possible.[23]

This is not the picture for Spanish-speaking immigrants, particularly Dominicans. Glenn Hendricks concludes that these recent immigrants tend to view the public schools with favor. Since mothers often work, the schools perform a much-needed child-care function, and learning English is seen as useful whether the family stays in the United States or returns to the

Caribbean to start a business. High school seems less useful because most of their youngsters can get work without it. Extended schooling is opposed for women. As is true for Mexican girls today and for Italians in years past, getting a high school education is a hard battle for Dominican girls, although it can be done, even celebrated. When the first girl in an extended Dominican family graduated from high school in New York, there was a gala fiesta, but in the midst of the party an uncle warned the new graduate to keep "the cultura Dominica," that is, to marry soon and not aim for a career.[24]

Some Dominican parents, when they can afford it, prefer to send their children to parochial schools, partly for religious reasons but mostly because they perceive public schools to be lax in terms of discipline. This is also the view of the newest Jewish immigrants, who are afraid that the New York City public schools will corrupt and possibly injure their children. Like the Dominicans in Washington Heights, therefore, some Russian Jews in Brooklyn send their youngsters to parochial schools, called *yeshivahs*. Most of the new entrants do not stay very long, however, because they are not willing to accept the religious rituals, which are entirely foreign to them and to their parents. After a difficult year, they usually return to the public schools, where they are helped to adjust via bilingual programs.[25]

Newer Asian families, Chinese from Taiwan and Hong Kong, Koreans, Cambodians, and Vietnamese have attitudes similar to some of the earlier arrivals, such as the Jews. They value their children highly and undergo hardships so their offspring can obtain as much education as possible, partly because an educated child raises their own status in the community and partly because they see the connection between schooling and upward mobility. In regard to the latter point, the business unit of CUNY, Baruch College, among others, such as Queens College and City College, have enrolled thousands of students from recently arrived Chinese families. In many cases, unfortunately, parental aspirations cannot be met because bilingualism and poorly defined criteria for high school graduation fail to prepare their children for college work.[26]

Many Asian youngsters are also enrolled in after-school and weekend classes to reinforce their knowledge of the language spoken in their homes and to acquaint them with their native culture. As is true for other groups, Asian parents want to be able to communicate with their children and to keep the traditions of their homeland alive. Chinese language classes, when combined with bilingual public schools classes, may, however, retard children's ability to learn English.[27]

In spite of coming at different times and from different places, immigrant parents seem to have shared some similar attitudes toward public schools. For one thing, for all but their youngest children, formal education was a luxury, because at least in the first generation most immigrant families were poor. Also, although for different reasons, many foreign-born parents feared public schools, some because they thought secular education would diminish their children's religious faith, others because they thought it would distance their children from them, making their children "real" Americans while the remained mired in hard labor and poverty, "greenhorns," unable to communicate with their Yankee offspring. In addition, there were parents who feared that physical harm would come to their children from hostile peers in other groups, while still others worried about moral corruption, especially of their daughters. To the extent that they saw formal education as a road to higher income and status, they were able to submerge their fears and encourage their youngsters to go to school. When they did not make this connection, they and their children became enemies of public education. Which parents were right? Which were wrong? A look at the school experiences of immigrant children, even if they attended for only a short time, may settle the issue.

Experiences

Immigrant children from Northern and Western Europe—Irish, Germans, Jewish and otherwise, Danes, Norwegians, and Swedes—who arrived in the middle of the nineteenth century shared a common educational experience. Wherever their parents settled, public schools were either nonexistent or inadequate, and as a result most of these youngsters attended some kind of private school. The elaborate public school systems established in urban areas later in the nineteenth century were not available to the Irish who came to the East Coast cities in the 1830s and 1840s, and tax-supported rural schools were not plentiful in most of the newly settled communities chosen for settlement by immigrant families from Germany or Scandinavia.

The nature of the schools the new arrivals entered varied with the place to which their parents had brought them. German and Irish children in New York City would probably attend, at least for a few years, a charity school operated by the Public School Society or the Children's Aid Society, both of which were free. In Boston, a Catholic child would enroll in one of many parochial schools. After 1842 a public school system was in place in the Empire City, but a child who moved from a charity school to one of the new ward schools would hardly know the difference. Whether the schools were free or charged a fee, as was the case with the small but growing number of parochial schools, the methods and course of study were similar. All, to save money, used the Lancastrian or monitorial system, in which a teenaged monitor would be responsible for a dozen or so younger children and one adult teacher ruled from on high. Students learned the "three Rs" by rote and endured harsh discipline and sometimes—as for the Irish—a fair amount of bigotry. Possibly as a result, most children left school early.[28]

The public school system that resulted from the first of New York City's great school wars led to the creation of primary and grammar schools in each of the 22 wards into which the city was then divided. The former were for children at least five years old, and their function was to teach basic skills. In primary school a child was expected to learn simple arithmetic and to complete the first five reading books. The small number of immigrant children who went on to grammar school were expected to complete four additional readers and build on the rudimentary skills learned earlier.[29]

Teaching methods and basic content were the same in any of the schools a young Irish or German child might attend, but there were other differences. Parochial schools, for example, used part of the school day for religious instruction, which caused them to forgo subjects such as nature study and manual training, present in some of the secular schools. The Children's Aid Society schools de-emphasized academic work and tried to teach a trade, but their efforts were not well received. In their Third Annual Report in 1856, for example, the trustees discussed their failure to keep German immigrant girls in one of their Lower East Side schools. The total enrollment in this particular school was 235, but the average daily attendance was only 97. The school provided dinner and shoes and clothing when needed, but, as a newspaper article of the time stated, "not one in a hundred [German families] ever send their children to school." According to the "home visitor" employed by Children's Aid to get more students into its schools, the children themselves wanted to stay in school, but their parents wanted them to earn money.[30]

Several areas of the South attracted German Jewish immigrants—Atlanta, Georgia, for one. In the 1840s that city used tax money only for schooling indigent children, and most Jews did not fall in that category. At that early date the Jewish community was not able to establish schools of its own, so Jewish youngsters attended private academies along with Gentile children. One such boy, Herman Levi, recalled being taught English from a German fable translated into "American words."[31]

Public schools were available in rural Iowa, but most of the Danish families who settled there tried to avoid them and built their own bicultural schools, where children were taught the Danish language and culture as well as English. As was often the case, the financial burden proved too great, and these all-day schools were gradually converted into Saturday schools.[32] Norwegian children living farther west in the Dakota Territory went to a community school that was 16-by-16 feet square, made of round logs chinked with plaster, and had no ceiling. The roof was covered with elm bark, and the room had two windows, a door, and a stove. The schoolmaster said there was "plenty of firewood and he made no attempt to economize." It was an ungraded school, so the children were of "all ages and sizes," but he made sure to put the youngest nearest the stove.[33]

In many urban neighborhoods, immigrant children outnumbered the native-born by far. As Betty Smith relates in her autobiographical novel about an Irish American family in the immigrant-laden Williamsburg section of Brooklyn, her heroine, Francie Nolan, was the only child in her class with native-born parents. Because this was so rare, she had a difficult time convincing her teacher that she was telling the truth.[34] At other schools in New York City the population was less homogeneous. The register books of Grammar School 14, a boys' school located on Twenty-seventh Street between Second and Third Avenues, contain information regarding parental nativity and occupations for the 12,000 students enrolled between 1835 and 1866. The records indicate that at this school, located in a lower-middle-class area, boys whose fathers had been born in Ireland, Germany, England, and Scotland attended in accord with their incidence in the eligible population. What accounts for the difference in enrollment patterns is the length of time the family had lived in New York, information also listed in the register books. Those in America long enough to have native-born, school-age children had been able to leave the ethnic enclaves housing the more recently arrived.[35]

In 1908, the U.S. Immigration Commission listed 21 cities in which the percentage of children with foreign-born parents who were in school was greater than those with native-born parents. Most were in the Northeast or north central states; only in San Francisco was this duplicated. The commission investigators were extremely thorough. In the same volume they connected specific groups of foreign-born children with particular cities. Russian Polish Jews, for example, made up 33 percent of the New York City school population, Germans constituted 32 percent in Milwaukee, and the Irish dominated school statistics in Boston and Lowell, Massachusetts. The Portuguese did the same in New Bedford, another Massachusetts town, as did the Swedes in Minneapolis and Duluth.[36]

Most of the schools in these cities were not prepared for the influx of children but took them in anyway, leading to dreadful overcrowding. Teachers in the largest immigrant-receiving cities often wished that some of the newcomers would wait before coming to school and bemoaned the fact that the immigrant children who landed on Saturday and settled in on Sunday appeared in their jam-packed classrooms on Monday.

In New York City at the turn of the century, classes of 60–70 were the rule. The principal of Public School 75, which had a virtually all-Jewish population, enlarged his enrollment by 500 children, but another 500 children and parents created a small riot outside the school when he was forced to say no more could be admitted.[37] One student in such a school told an interviewer many years later that she had to sit in the same seat with another girl and put her arm around her seatmate's waist "so that I shouldn't fall off on the other side." Many schools resorted to part-time scheduling, so that a child might receive only half of a usual education. In addition, schools in immigrant neighborhoods were often very old and unsafe. Italian youngsters in South Philadelphia, for example, attended schools without indoor toilets or play space.[38]

To their credit, most cities tried to build enough schools to meet the new needs. In New York City a gifted architect, C. B. Snyder, presided over the construction of 38 new elementary schools between 1899 and 1914; the first three Manhattan and Bronx high schools were also erected during this period. Each of the new schools contained more light and air as well as specialized rooms for cooking, manual-training classes, and physical education. Many also included rooftop areas where children with symptoms of tuberculosis were taught by a teacher as thoroughly bundled up as her charges, who reclined in deck chairs and blankets like passengers on a cruise ship.[39] A new school in a Boston immigrant enclave, the North End, which was named after Paul Revere, included shower baths, considered a necessity because many Italian mothers followed an Old World custom of swaddling their children in woolen rags during cold weather. Attempts to cut them free brought loud cries of "Don't do that! My momma got me tied up for the winter!"[40]

Some children, of course, had to attend older schools, and this might have been a reason why they disliked school. Italian youngsters in Chicago told whoever asked that they had many unpleasant classroom experiences, physical and otherwise, that made them leave early. Teachers and principals, they said, constantly mispronounced their names, to "the amused tittering" of their classmates.[41] Other Italian children had different complaints. Misled by Italian prowess in the arts, teachers had high expectations regarding their performance in music and drawing, and when the children could not live up to what was expected, they were punished and degraded. As author Jerre Mangione said, "We were expected to be particularly brilliant in Latin and . . . the Romance languages and as to music and drawing, our teachers were positively insulted if we did not show signs of becoming another Verdi or another Da Vinci".[42] An interview with a former principal of a school in Little Italy, New York, indicated an additional reason for the stress on artistic studies. Italian children, he said, were difficult to teach and control. Giving up on the three Rs, in some cases teachers would arrange for them to spend most of their school day in music and art classes or at the gymnasium and the playground. During the first two decades of heavy Italian immigration, elementary school methods and curricula were so unsuitable that some observers "wondered what was to be gained by an immigrant child who attended."[43]

There was really no reason to expect these children from the poorest areas of southern Italy and Sicily to be Michaelangelos, but one instructor in the Newark, New Jersey, schools found a way to use the great artist's name to win over her rambunctious class. She read them the story of Michaelangelo, and her pupils loved it. "Every Michael, every Angelo, every relation of a Michael or an Angelo basked in the wonderful feeling of kinship with the great master."[44] Not all teachers were able or willing to be as ingenious as this young woman, and as a result many children remembered school as an unpleasant experience. Teaching methods had not changed very much since the Lancastrian days; learning was still a matter of memorization and drill. In one of his first days at school, Leonard Covello recalled "sitting in a class trying to memorize words written on the blackboard, words which had absolutely no meaning to me because the teacher had never explained them." Covello said he learned penmanship and spelling by "painfully and carefully copying a misspelled word ten times or more in his 'blankbook.'" He also studied other subjects by the same method, repetition.[45]

Other children at other schools had their own reasons for disliking school. An elderly woman who came to Homestead, Pennsylvania, from Eastern Europe as a nine year old went to school for the first time and had a difficult experience. She knew no English and was therefore unable to understand what anyone around her was saying. Her classmates "laughed at her, called her names and shoved her around." She left school in the fourth grade and went to work as a domestic.[46] This youngster would have had an easier time of it in a school where there were many foreigners, especially if they were from the same ethnic group. This was certainly the case in the larger cities, but even when they had the protection of numbers, many children found school unpleasant, as Sol Levine remembered from his school days in New York: "I had a fourth grade teacher, Miss Peterson. She wasn't a good teacher. She hit us with a pointer if we talked at the wrong time. . . . Most of the time I got hit for reading under the desk. . . . She struck us left and right. She induced us to be bad; she hollered, she bullied us."[47]

An elderly woman recalled an even more painful incident, when she needed to use the bathroom and the teacher embarrassed and humiliated her because she had failed to ask permission properly, that is, saying "may I leave the room," instead of "can." Many children remembered the annoyance of weekly examinations for head lice and their teacher's frequent criticism of their clothes. On occasion, the instructor in a school that lacked the bathing facitiies of the Paul Revere School would send a note recommending more frequent baths, to which one immigrant mother in Cleveland responded, "Maria is not a rose, do not smell her, teach her!"[48]

Classes established for the children who spoke no English were, of course, of the greatest importance, because knowledge of the language of instruction was basic to everything else. New York City in the 1890s had the most foreign-born children and so provided the most opportunities to learn English. In classes labeled "C," children were totally immersed in English, punished if they used their native tongue, and separated from their English-speaking peers. If they survived the ordeal, they were placed after six months or at most a year in classes more or less appropriate to their age group. If they could not make the grade, they joined other failures in "D" classes and, as expected, dropped out early. A small group of children, usually older, who did very well during the immersion process moved to "E" classes, which used an accelerated curriculum to bring them up to their peers by the end of the eighth grade.[49]

Some version of this system was also in place in other cities. Chicago, for example, had "beginner's classes" similar to the "C" classes used in New York. But in Chicago the classes were offered only in the fall. Non-English-speaking youngsters arriving during the winter or the spring had to wait until the next year to enter school. In Boston the situation was better. There, so-called ungraded classes provided the first school experience for children who spoke no English. One teacher, using "quiet, pleasant tones" first taught them the words for basic class routines: "rise, file, pencil," etc., before going on to more abstract words. Boston also had a version of New York's "D" classes, called "special difficulty" classes, for children not likely to stay in school to the eighth grade.[50]

For a variety of reasons, including the desire to keep immigrant children in school as long as possible, public schools in all the cities with large foreign populations were, in Lawrence Cremin's word, "transformed." In Cleveland, for example, the Murray Hill School, built to accommodate Italian immigrant children, provided services such as special classes, medical examinations, and nursing services. This new school also had a rooftop classroom, a swimming pool, a dental dispensary, and a model home. The latter was meant to make girls eager to make such a home for themselves. This unusual institution also employed an Italian to teach the language and encouraged the music teacher to play Italian songs. In New York, the superintendent of schools, in a desperate move to improve Italian school attendance, hired an Italian-speaking truant officer.[51]

The effects of the Murray Hill School were rarely duplicated. Some of what it offered, however, was also present in other urban schools attended by many immigrant children. Nature study, for example, deemed important for children living in an urban slum, was introduced into the elementary course of study in several cities, and in many schools, attention was paid to the non-English-speaking child, the slow learner, and the gifted. Other social services, such as the free-lunch program previously mentioned, were also part of the effort to create schools that would suit the needs of immigrant children. Schooling, however, was not a one-way street, and on occasion the immigrant children would bring their own experiences into the classroom. When a teacher in a Lower East Side New York school asked her charges what "the Americans who could no longer put up with the abuse of the English should have done, a young girl from a working class family said 'go on strike!'"[52]

In spite of the efforts of school boards and superintendents, some children never liked school. The difficulty of learning a new language in addition to geography, arithmetic, and other such subjects was "a heavy burden for the children who could not connect their studies with their home lives." Even if they were bright and learned quickly, those who were in the minority had other difficulties. They were "nervous from nine to three, ridiculed for the clothes they wore" and the food they ate. One boy, fearful of his classmates, disposed of the pepper and onion sandwich brought from home as soon as he could. Other youngsters, particularly girls, at least in retrospect, spoke of adoring school. Much seemed to depend on their teachers.[53] In any case, however, in the late nineteenth and early twentieth centuries, the child's response to his or her school experience was not the determinant of how long it lasted. Outside influences, notably economic, were more likely to determine the length of an immigrant child's school career.

To what extent are the experiences of the past valid for the newer immigrant groups? The severity varies, but all, to a greater or lesser extent, have adjustment problems. The children of Cuban refugees in Florida do not share the interests of their Americanized peers in sports or other extracurricular activities, and young Russian Jews find the ways of American schools strange. As one said in an interview, "it's very hard to adjust when you come from a radically different country, when your first language [and] your way of thinking about the world is radically different from those of your classmates."[54]

Haitian children have enormous difficulty in the schools. Conflict with their black American classmates and free and open classroom discussions—as opposed to the memorization customary in Haitian schools—are just some of the problems. The largest group of newcomers, the Chinese, are having a complex experience. Those from Hong Kong find English easier to master, but using the language of their new homeland is generally very difficult. In a Chinatown New York elementary school in 1979, one third of the children spoke English well, one third hesitantly, and one third poorly. Those in a second area of settlement, Elmhurst, Queens, did better; 62 percent spoke English well, 26 percent hesitantly, and only 12 percent poorly. All schools report that Chinese youngsters do well in mathematics and attend regularly.[55]

In 1991, 121,177 students in New York City elementary schools were described as having "limited English proficiency," and as a result the board of education now operates bilingual programs in Spanish (the largest), Chinese, Haitian, Creole, Korean, Russian, Vietnamese, French, Greek, Arabic, Khmer, and Italian. Chicago does even more, employing teachers who speak 20 of the 110 different languages spoken in the schools. Few cities are able to manage and afford such large programs, but as a result of the 1974 Supreme Court decision stating that children must be educated in a language they can understand, they must do as much as they can.[56]

Much of the money for these special programs comes from a federal program that pays for extra tutoring and classes aimed at low-achieving children. To get the aid, which depends on the number of poor children on their registers, the schools present applications for free lunch as proof of poverty. In many districts these arrangements work well, but in areas densely populated with newly arrived immigrants from countries where their every move was scrutinized by authorities, it is difficult; these people do not want to give any information about themselves (especially if they are undocumented aliens) on a government form. The result is that some schools with a large enrollment of immigrant children do not get the money for much needed programs. In New York, for example, the East Harlem school district, which has many immigrants from Mexico and Central America, or Prospect Heights in Brooklyn, where three fourths of the students are immigrants, mostly from the Caribbean, officials are often unable to get the 1,500 lunch applications they need for the school to qualify. Other immigrant-receiving cities, such as Miami, Boston, Los Angeles, and Houston, have the same problem.[57]

It is not clear whether bilingual programs are being used as intended, that is, as a way for foreign-born children to keep up with their academic courses while learning English, or whether they become a permanent alternative to learning English. What is clear is that while not all Asian youngsters are successful in school, their presence in selective high schools and colleges on both coasts seems to show a better experience with formal education than many of the immigrant children who came before them.

According to sociologist Aubrey Bonnett, for West Indian children from the English-speaking Caribbean islands, "entrance into and coping with the city's public educational system can be a nightmare." Their heavy accents are difficult for American teachers and students to understand, leading them to be passed over by the instructors and ridiculed by other children. "The net result is that they develop a poor self image . . . and ultimately develop negative attitudes to school and learning."[58]

In California, the schools in Los Angeles County and the children and teachers in them are having a very difficult time because the schools are being asked to assume the difficult task of bridging the gap between the Third World and America for many newcomers. Between 1969 and 1985, the percentage of Hispanic children in the Los Angeles County schools grew from 20.8 percent to 49.1 percent, some from Central America and the Caribbean but most from Mexico. No other school system in the United States has ever experienced such a concentrated influx of students from a single foreign country. One result of this has been severely overcrowded schools in primarily Hispanic areas of the city.[59]

This is also the picture in New York's Chinatown. In one school, where 90 percent of the children are Chinese, there are 1,100 children in a building meant to house 914. In spite of the crowding, however (the school lunch-room runs double shifts for breakfast and lunch), daily attendance averages 95 percent. Although many Chinese children like school, others do not and would gladly not attend. Their complaints include: "I don't like reading English. English is so confusing. There are too many grammar rules." Another found the school day in New York to be too long; in Hong Kong they went to school for only half a day. Still another stated his feeling sim-ply: "I don't like school . . . I wish we could back to Hong Kong." A Hmong boy, Pao, echoed this boy's sentiment, saying that he didn't like school because it was too hard. Unlike the Chinese youngster, however, Pao had no desire to return to Indochina, where his ethnic group had suffered terrible hardships.[60]

Earlier traumas affect the behavior of many immigrant children who have come to the United States as refugees from civil war and its accompa-nying terrors. An eight-year-old girl from El Salvador, for example, con-stantly fought with her classmates. Her guidance counselor believed that her disruptive actions were the result of having seen her father shot dead by government troops. There was also trauma resulting from difficult and dan-gerous trips. A 10-year-old boy from Vietnam never spoke in class because he had been crowded into a tiny boat and "forced not to cry for fear of alerting enemies." Cambodian children who have witnessed violence when their country was in the hands of Pol Pot have terrible nightmares. Many never attended school because during the years that his party, the Khmer Rouge, ruled, children and parents were imprisoned in camps where there was no school at all.[61]

Truly, these youngsters have a formidable task before them, complicated by the fact that their teachers know very little about Cambodian culture. According to a report on the newest immigrants, *New Voices,* in Cambodia hand gestures are used to call dogs and are seen as rude behavior. When American teachers beckon to their charges or applaud them, or use their hands in other ways, Cambodian youngsters are offended. Crossing one's fingers for luck, an ordinary American gesture, is seen as obscene by the Cambodians.[62]

One teacher told an interviewer about a child who came to school each day and who understood the class when numbers were involved but other-wise just sat at his desk looking "politely miserable." At a different school, which did not have a bilingual program, a 10-year-old immigrant boy was placed in the slowest class for his grade. He got very discouraged and became disruptive when he made no progress and could not keep up with his grade.[63]

A 1985 study estimates that 3.5–5.5 million children in the United States have limited English proficiency (LEP), a figure that is certainly much larger today. More than 100,000 of such children lived in New York City in 1984, with the next largest group in Los Angeles.[64] Since 1974, federal law requires that programs improving educational performance be established for all schools with a sizable number of children who are economically deprived (receive benefits from Aid to Dependent Families with Children [ADFC] or whose family income is below the poverty level); who are "educationally deprived, culturally deprived," or "disadvantaged"; or have limited English proficiency.[65]

As in New York City, most schools have opted for bilingual programs in which the children study most subjects in their native language and are also taught English. In theory, this allows the LEP child to keep up with the regular curriculum for his or her age group while learning English. Other schools prefer programs in which a student gets heavy doses of English while also studying other subjects with English-speaking peers.[66] Different cities offer special opportunities specific to immigrant children. In Brownsville, Texas, for example, Mexican or other Hispanic children who feel ill can see a bilingual school nurse. San Francisco has established a Newcomer High School that has 39 different nationalities in the student body. New York has a Liberty High School in which native languages from Albanian to Urdu are heard.[67]

Current efforts stand in stark contrast to programs used in the past. Until the start of the twentieth century, non-English-speaking children, regardless of age, were placed in first grade. As William H. Maxwell, the New York City superintendent of schools said in 1912: "It is absurd to place the boy or girl, 10 or 12 years of age, just landed from Italy, who cannot read a word in his own language or speak a word of English, in the same classroom with American boys and girls five or six years old."[68] Maxwell said this in his annual report to justify the program he had begun some years earlier, and as a result of his initiative, in most of the larger cities, immigrant children began to receive special attention.

As we have seen, the usual procedure was to place non-English-speaking children, regardless of age, in a separate class for five or six months and then transfer them to the grade where, if age was used as the criterion, they appropriately belonged. During the brief period in which they were in the special class, they were immersed in English, indeed they were forbidden to use their native language anywhere on school grounds. The aim of the teacher was to get the youngsters to express themselves in English. One instructor gave an example: "They learn the names of objects, occupations and allied words and how to apply them properly." The methods included drill "en masse" on pronunciation and much body movement on the part of the teacher as she illustrated the words she was trying to teach. As the nicknames for the classes "steamer" or "vestibule" indicate, they were meant to be as temporary as possible. They were limited to children more than eight years old. If they were younger, it was expected that they could manage in a regular class. Furthermore, since there was never enough room, they were admitted according to need. Children over eight with no European education got first preference, partially educated and over eight came second.[69]

Regardless of how well children did in the special class, after six months at most they were left to sink or swim in a regular class. The permissible age for leaving school for most of this period was 17, and those immigrant children for whom total immersion had not worked very well left at the first opportunity and, as we shall see, were truants before they departed. Others, probably because they were literate in some language, remained at least until the eighth grade, and some even went on to high school.

Are the newer teaching techniques working better? If we look at length of stay, the answer is yes, but this is largely a function of raising the permissible age for leaving school. If we look at the number of children who began their schooling with a language handicap and have gone to high school and college, we should be further encouraged. Unfortunately, however, this apparent success is more the result of lower standards for grading, promotion, and graduation, not evidence of learning. A contemporary study of bilingual education in Los Angeles found that classes were poorly staffed with teachers who had a vested interest in keeping their charges in a bilingual class as long as possible and that graduates of these classes dropped out of high school much more frequently than their English-speaking peers.[70]

This evaluation applies to other cities where bilingual education has become a substitute for regular education rather than the gateway that was originally intended. In New York City, at the high school that most Chinese students attend, Seward Park, attendance is poor and the drop-out rate is high: 45 percent of the students speak English well, but 41 percent speak it hesitantly and 13 percent speak it poorly. Perhaps even more telling, more than half of the students entering the City University of New York fail to pass the reading and writing assessment tests administered at entry and require, in many cases, several semesters of remediation.[71]

There is also another fairly recent development, in effect in many schools, which reinforces the idea that bilingualism is not the answer to the problem of preparing the child with limited English proficiency for life in the mainstream. Special education programs, funded by state and federal money, were begun in the 1970s, reflecting larger concerns about disadvantaged children. Originally intended for the physically and mentally handicapped, their number has grown and resulted in a sort of "school deportation" under which all sorts of children who are difficult to teach, including those whose only handicap is not knowing much English, are shunted.[72]

Comparisons with the past are difficult. Prior to 1971, when the City University reduced its entry requirements, only the best and the brightest of New York City high school graduates attended. If similar standards were applied today, very few graduates of the bilingual programs would be admitted. As things stand now, most professors who teach youngsters whose first language was not English find that bilingualism as currently practiced in New York has not achieved the intended results.

Usage

An examination of the extent to which schools were used by the children of immigrants—that is, how many enrolled, how long they stayed, how often they attended, how much they learned—reveals both differences and similarities. In general, German children, possibly because many of their schools were "user friendly," used them more than the Irish, who arrived at approximately the same time. French Canadians in New England used them even less. Eastern European Jewish children appeared to stay in school longer than Italians. Bohemians and Scandinavian youngsters remained in the schoolroom for more years than Mexican children, and today Chinese and Japanese children are more likely to be long-term students than children from the Caribbean and Central America. Cultural differences are responsible for most of the variations; poverty for the similarities. Most immigrants of every group were poor and needed the income a child could earn. For this reason, older children of any group were likely to spend fewer years in school than their younger siblings. Many children never went to school at all because the educational authorities never knew they existed.

In spite of such bureaucratic slippage, however, most children of the foreign-born did attend school for at least the primary grades. The time of their arrival made a big difference. As we have seen, compulsory education laws did not exist when the Irish came; partly as a result, in 1852 only 58 percent of the children in one of Boston's most homogeneously Irish wards were enrolled in any kind of school. Four years later, in another heavily Irish district, only 50 percent were in the schoolroom. This trend persisted. In the same district—the North End—the graduating class of the local grammar school was for many years only a small part of the group that had originally enrolled. In most years, out of 200 who entered perhaps 50 graduated. The sharpest drop came between the seventh and eight grades, when most children turned 14. Probably because there would have been few takers, the North End had no high school. In 1856, in another heavily Irish district, only 50 percent of the eligible children were in school.[73] The percentage in an Irish district in Pittsburgh four years later was only eight points higher. At approximately the same time in New York, the Catholic schools, almost all attended by Irish youngsters, were able to educate less than 20 percent of those eligible, and almost none stayed to the eighth grade. In Providence, Rhode Island, in 1880, most children entered school at six or seven and remained to 13, but the Irish dropped out earlier. Only 68 percent of those whose parents were born in the Emerald Isle were in school at 13, while 80 percent of all Providence children of the same age were in the classroom.[74]

One group of immigrant children, those from French-speaking Canadian families who were employed in the mills and factories in Maine and other areas of northern New England, were able to keep their sons and daughters working by telling a prospective employer that their child was older than he or she really was. If the school authorities became aware of this and tried to get the children into the classroom, the whole family moved to another district where they were not known and kept the children working. Other devices used to evade compulsory education laws, where they existed, did not require moving. A son or daughter who was taller than the norm and, as was true for many of the children who were born abroad, had no birth or baptismal papers was declared by parents to be old enough to work. In the absence of documents to the contrary, the authorities did not press the issue. Even German children in St. Louis, whose parents, as we have seen, valued education enough to fight for the schools they wanted, ended their school careers early.[75]

In the late nineteenth and early twentieth centuries, owing in part to the great increase in immigration, the length of schooling of the child of foreign-born parents became a more pressing issue. "Wherever school men and women looked . . . they saw the children of immigrants." In 1911, 57.8 percent of all the pupils in the 37 cities investigated by the U.S. Immigration Commission, a congressional body that produced a 42-volume report on immigrants, were the children of foreign-born parents. In New York, 71.5 percent of the 500,000 children attending school had foreign-born fathers. In Duluth, 74.1 percent were of foreign-born parents, and in Cleveland, Cincinnati, Detroit, Minneapolis, Buffalo, Boston, San Francisco, and most other large cities, 40 percent of all children in schools had foreign-born parents.[76]

Because most the new arrivals knew no English, they were in the primary grades (one to three), although they were much older than the normal age (six to eight) for those beginning classes. As a result, they would reach the usual age for leaving school, as young as 10 in some states, with a very limited school experience. The Immigration Commission found that in 1908, 36 percent of 10-, 11-, and 12-year-old foreign-born children in the 12 cities they examined were "retarded" in school progress. Robert Woods, a settlement-house worker in Boston in 1903, said that "the graduating class of a grammar school is a small part of the children who entered six years before."[77]

Whether a boy or girl was in the proper grade or not, being listed on the class register did not mean that he or she was in classroom. Two social workers, Edith Abbott and Sophinisba Breckenridge, made a detailed study of nonattendance in Chicago in 1917 and found that 63 percent of the children in a heavily Italian West Side school were absent on a given day, and a similar percentage, 61 percent, were absent from a North Side school, used mostly by Polish children. Other parts of their study refer to Chicago immigrants as a whole. Abbott and Breckenridge found that from September 1911 to May 1915, 60 percent of the foreign-born children who should have been in school were not.[78]

Two years earlier, in 1915, the figures were even worse for immigrant children whose parents had settled in small Illinois towns. In such places, almost 80 percent of the eligible youths were absent from the classroom. This data was compiled by the Immigrants Protective League, which in 1911 began to act as a clearinghouse "by obtaining from the federal immigration authorities the names of all arriving children of compulsory school age" whose documents showed that they were bound for Illinois. The league then sent the names to the various localities to which the children had gone, and, usually, although not always, the local school authorities tried to get them enrolled.[79]

Illness was often the cause of absence but much more important was the need for the income a child could earn. Aware of this but at the same time enormously concerned with the danger inherent in an undereducated foreign-born population, the "child savers"—that is, progressive reformers—launched a campaign for "more effective and stringent school attendance laws." This attitude was based at least in part on what one historian calls the "Christian work ethic." Strongly against child labor on moral grounds and even more opposed to idleness, reformers wanted as long a period of compulsory education as they could possibly get.[80]

There had been demands for such a law in New York since the 1860s, and the state legislature passed such an act in 1874. It required children to attend school from age 8 to 12, but it was not effective because it only required a parent to say that the child was 12 to get permission for him or her to go to work. After many years of lobbying for a stronger law, the settlement-house leaders forced the New York State Legislature to authorize a school census so that the dimensions of the problem could be known. The results showed that almost 150,000 children within the stated age limits were not in any kind of school. The information had the desired effect, and in 1897 an addition to the basic law said that a youngster could not get working papers unless he or she had attended school for at least 80 days before his or her twelfth birthday. Superintendent Maxwell, however, was not satisfied, and with the support of the New York Child Labor Committee he succeeded, in 1903, raising the school-leaving age to 14.[81]

Enforcement, however, remained a problem. Because it was difficult to achieve compliance, many reformers tried other means of getting children, especially foreign children, to enroll and remain in school. As we have seen, the Immigrants Protective League had tried to send the names of new arrivals to the Illinois communities in which they planned to live. Other ideas were also tried. In New York, the Committee on Truancy of the New York City Teachers Council proposed translating the nonattendance notices that were mailed to parents into Italian, Yiddish, and German. Another plan introduced in New York and also in Philadelphia and Boston was to use a "school visitor," usually but not always a woman, to visit the homes of nonattendees and try to solve the problem that was keeping the boy or girl out of school. This approach was pioneered by the settlement-house workers in the poorest sections of several cities, but they never had enough money, and language barriers prevented successful communication with parents.[82]

Still another approach was to establish industrial schools, on the theory that if skills were taught both children and parents would see more reason to attend school. Settlement personnel argued that industrial training enlivened the school day and brought the children more real-life experiences. Most parents, themselves working with their hands, liked such classes, as did their children. Clearly, this kind of training had the potential to reduce truancy because it was expected to make school so attractive that "the children would not willingly be absent."[83]

Maybe so. The obstacles, however, were many. Often there were genuine emergencies. Robert Woods, working in the North End of Boston, said that "a drunken mother, a dying baby sister," and two working parents (leading them to thrust the care of some half-dozen younger children on the shoulders of a boy or girl of 12) were some of the reasons given to truant officers who investigated nonattendance. Another reason reflects a problem discussed earlier. In cities where there were no "steamer" or "vestibule" classes, older non-English-speaking children were miserable in classes with little ones. As one told the attendance officer: "I'm too big to be in first grade."[84]

As a general rule, a child who was almost 14 simply ignored school, and no truant officer called once it was understood that he or she would leave in a few months. Sometimes a child would come to school and be sent home again "to rid himself of vermin." Embarrassed and angry, he or she did not come back. Teachers sometimes alienated parents. An Italian mother brought her son to school after beating him for "playing hooky" and received only angry criticism from his instructor for her efforts. For all these reasons, exacerbated by the lack of sufficient truant officers and the inadequacy of those available, immigrant children were often absent from school.[85]

So much for elementary school. As would be expected, fewer foreign-born children attended grammar school (grades six to nine) and only a small number went to high school. In Providence in 1908 less than 10 percent of the Italian children, as compared with 40 percent of rest of the city's children, were in high school. In 1915, the statistics indicated little improvement: 95 percent of Italian sons aged 15 or older and 78 percent of Italian daughters of the same age were at work, not at school. Much the same picture was true in Cleveland. Compared with Romanian and Slovak young-sters, many fewer children from Italian families remained beyond the ninth grade.[86]

David Hogan constructed a table based on data in a 1922 report com-piled by the Department of Vocational Guidance of the Chicago Board of Education. Responses to a questionnaire administered to 596 eighth-grade children in a "highly congested poor immigrant area of the city in which many nationalities were represented" showed that only 49 of the 84 Bohemian youngsters questioned, 54 of the 92 Italians, and 18 of the 31 Poles intended to go to high school. More Jewish teenagers planned to extend their education, but even in this group only 102 of the 126 boys and girls interviewed planned to do so. Matters improved somewhat in the 1920s. Nationwide, there was a 20 percent increase in high school enroll-ment of foreign-born children aged 14–15 and a 28 percent increase for those 16–18.[87]

Speaking about immigrant children as a whole in the early twentieth century, John Bodnar found that while 60 percent of native-born white chil-dren began high school, less than a third of the German and less than a quar-ter of the Italians did so. He also found that by 1910, less than 10 percent of the Italian, Polish, and Slovak children stayed beyond the sixth grade in Buffalo, Chicago, and Cleveland. A different study found this to be true in New York City as well, and those that did enroll left before completion. In 1958, an investigation of the educational level attained by Italian parents indicated that most had not gone past the sixth grade. John Briggs found that this was also the case in the Italian colonies in Utica and Rochester, New York. In 1926, according to Leonard Covello, when an Italian family might have been in New York for 40 years, only 11 percent of Italian Americans graduated from the Empire City's high schools. Thomas Churchill found this to be true in Newark, New Jersey, 16 years later, and Gary Mormino said the same percentage would be accurate for Italian males over 25 in St. Louis at approximately the same time.[88]

If we look at the length of schooling of the Eastern European Jewish immigrants, we find that prior to World War I, it was the sons of German Jews, products of an earlier immigration, who were using education to enter the professions. Russian and Polish Jews, although they remained in school longer than other immigrant children, were not yet doing so. The College of the City of New York (CCNY), which educated the bulk of the New York Eastern European sons later in the twentieth century, graduated at most 200 students a year by 1913 and conferred about the same number of degrees, mostly on young men from German Jewish families, for the next two decades. The sons of Russian and Polish Jews were enrolling in urban high schools all over the nation in larger numbers than other immigrant progeny as early as 1908 and were the second most likely group to stay for two years, but 71 percent failed to finish the course. A similar pattern applied to Eastern European Jewish youngsters in elementary schools. Compared with other immigrant groups, more enrolled, but compared with the school population as a whole, they did not stay as long.[89]

Personal stories reflect this. Philip Roth, in a *New York Times* editorial appearing in connection with the publication of his 1992 book, *Patrimony*, describes his father as the middle child in a family of seven whose immigrant parents were penniless on arrival and therefore unable to do without the wages he could earn after completing the eighth grade. Like others in his generation, Roth's father remained unschooled and undereducated. Rose Schneiderman became a prominent labor leader in 1909–11, but had only a sixth-grade education. To get even this much schooling had been difficult because her father died when she was nine years old and her mother had to go to work, leaving Rose at home to take care of her younger siblings.[90]

A young woman from another Jewish family benefited from the fact that she had been born later than her older sisters, who had been sent out to work at 12 while she was able to stay in school until she was 15. Eva Rubinstein Dizenfeld arrived in the United States when she was eight years old and spent only two years in school before going to work as a tobacco stripper. A Jewish man in Pittsburgh explained that he was unable to attend school for very long because his father bought a house and used his children's labor to convert it into apartments, which he then rented to other immigrants.[91]

Similar regrets were undoubtedly felt by some Italian children who were compelled to leave school at an early age, but for others it may have come as a relief. Many immigrant children, depending on their age on arrival and the speed with which they learned English, were often two or more years older than their American-born classmates. In 1908, the Immigration Commission found that 42 percent of Jewish children and 64 percent of Italian youngsters were in that category. Other groups who were ready to leave because they were too far behind to catch up included French Canadians, Poles, and Slovaks. In spite of this, however, retardation, defined as "older than the normal age for his or her grade," was a lesser reason for limited school usage. For all the immigrant children who arrived before 1924, poverty took first place. As John Bodnar has said, "A relatively marginal existence made it very difficult to contemplate sacrificing the income children generated."[92]

David Hogan, studying school usage by Slavic children in Chicago in 1907, found that the percentage of their children in school increased dramatically as family income rose: 38.3 percent of those making $500 per year, 65.7 percent of those taking home $750, 83.2 percent of those earning $1,000, and 94.7 percent of those whose incomes exceeded $1,500 were able to keep their youngsters in the classroom. Another aspect of the relationship between children and family income is demonstrated in Hogan's observation that in the same year, 22 percent of the income of Slavic families in Chicago was earned by their children. Hogan said that the people he was studying "were prepared to make extraordinary sacrifices in order to purchase a home as a form of economic insurance against unemployment, underemployment and old age." Most were successful, but "the high levels of home ownership were associated with high rates of child labor and low rates of school attendance." In general, the longer a family had been in the United States, the higher its income and the longer its children stayed in school.[93]

What of the children who come to the United States today speaking Chinese, Korean, Japanese, Thai, Spanish, Creole, or Russian? It appears to be a mixed bag. Almost all, because of compulsory education laws, must remain in school until they are 16, but there are a number of differences in the extent to which they go further. The Japanese appear to use schooling the most. In the 1980s, 58 percent of the second generation and 90 percent of the third generation were attending a college or university. Most of them intended to become part of America's corporate or scientific community. Many Japanese youngsters, however, expected to return to Japan when their parents finished their assignments in the United States. Knowledge of American ways and fluency in English will be of great value in furthering their careers in their homeland.[94]

A much more numerous and permanent group from Asia, the Chinese, constitute the largest ethnic group of Asian students. From all the available evidence, they, more than any other group of current immigrants, have made the connection between formal schooling and white-collar occupations and the professions. As a result, they are very well represented at the City University of New York, the State University of New York, the University of California, and other, more prestigious institutions. To many observers, the Chinese, in company with other Asian students, seem to be a model minority. High grades on the SAT examinations, which strongly influence college entry, overrepresentations on the Harvard, Princeton, and Berkeley campuses, and high achievement in difficult areas such as science and mathematics have led to this widely accepted view.

In the Korean community, very small until the passage of the 1965 Immigration Act, children seem to follow an educational path similar to that of the Chinese and Japanese. Given the fact that only those with advanced education, needed skills, considerable amounts of money, or relatives who have already established themselves in the United States are eligible to enter, it would be very surprising to find out that the children of this group were not doing well in school. Unlike the young people of the immigrant groups that preceded them, they do not have to go to work to survive. This may also be true for some other Asian immigrant children—Thai, Cambodian, Vietnamese—but because these communities are still relatively small and recent, they have not yet been closely studied. Filipinos are another Asian group that has not been sufficiently examined, but available information seems to indicate that most are using both the elementary and high schools in the various West Coast communities where they have settled.

In terms of school usage, the position of Hispanic children stands in sad contrast to that of Asians. As a recent headline in the *New York Times* states, "The Hispanic Drop-Out Rate Stays High." Poverty is the major reason. Mexican farmworkers, for example, are poor, and their children can earn money as pickers. The growing numbers of Hispanic immigrants from Central America are equally poor and need every penny that an adolescent child can add to the family coffers. When we note that most Cuban children from middle-class families who have been here since the 1960s complete high school and that Puerto Rican youngsters whose families have lived on the mainland for several generations do the same, it appears that higher family income, often the result of having been in the United States for a long time, is perhaps the most important determinant of who drops out and who stays in.[95]

In 1980, only 25 percent of Mexican American youths graduated from high school as compared with 86 percent of American youths. In general, Mexican American youngsters drop out of school at a higher rate than the children of other Hispanic immigrants. A recent book, *Minority Status and Schooling,* says that newcomers from Central and South America do better— even though their schools are as deficient and crowded as those attended by Mexican children—because they have not endured the "long history of degradation by the Anglo world" that Mexicans have experienced. A movie that appeared in 1988, *Stand and Deliver,* illustrated this point. In the film, which is based on a true story, a Mexican American teacher, unlike the Anglo teachers who have taught the rowdy and underprepared adolescent class to which he is assigned, has high expectations for their success and transmits this confidence to them with positive results.[96]

Immigrants from the Dominican Republic have been coming to the United States in larger and larger numbers for the last 10 years and in many respects have adjusted well to their new environment. This is not true, however, in regard to their use of educational opportunities. Several explanations for this have been offered. School conditions, including the failure of bilingual programs to bring children whose first language is not English up to grade level, the negative influence of peers, and most of all the feeling that formal education will not bring them a better life, explain why so many of the young people in this segment of the Hispanic community turn their backs on schooling. They are, however, not the only group of Spanish-speaking immigrants to do this. As of 1990, 35 percent of all Hispanics aged 16–20 never received a high school diploma, compared with 12 percent of African Americans and 9 percent of whites.[97]

As the foregoing pages have demonstrated, the schooling of immigrant children, as in the past, continues to be a subject of major importance to American society. Multiculturalism has replaced Americanization, but English remains the majority language and knowledge remains the key to upward mobility. Furthermore, the job opportunities that had been available to undereducated youngsters in the past, discussed in the next chapter, are no longer present. In the absence of a better mechanism, the schools remain the best way to limit crime, homelessness, drug addiction, and the other fearsome problems that affect all Americans, long settled or newly arrived, in the United States today.

3

Work and Play

Work

Almost every immigrant family, regardless of when they came to the United States, needed help from their children. In some cases the assistance consisted of services in the home. Youngsters carried water, emptied slops, ran errands, did simple cooking, and cared for younger siblings. Their real importance however, was the work they did for money, outside the home. The Irish, as a group, were the neediest. In Boston between 1840 and 1880, "an employed laborer could not earn enough to maintain a family of four," and for that reason, a child's wages were "crucial for subsistence." And not just in Boston. In Lawrence, Massachusetts, in 1847 almost all the Irish children worked in the mills; only six regularly attended school. Child workers were often preferred over their unemployed fathers, which may have been true in any mill city where unskilled labor could be used. Children, after all, cost less to employ than adults.[1]

Because the wages of an unskilled father were "insufficient for even a modest standard of living," the economic margin of many Irish families did not improve until their children entered the labor market. For some this came very early. A letter home from an Irish immigrant in 1831 said, "children at six years old can work and get some money," and a help-wanted advertisement in the *New York Daily Tribune* in September 1850, when Irish immigration was at its peak, said jobs were waiting for "excellent" young children, recently arrived and ready to work for moderate wages. In Philadelphia at one point, Irish children contributed 65 percent of the total family income.[2]

In another "Little Dublin," Fall River, Massachusetts, in 1879, 25 percent of the mill workers were under 15, most of them Irish. As late as 1908 they contributed 45 percent of their family's income. By that date, Massachusetts prohibited child labor by children younger than 14 and required a certificate of minimal school completion for children 14–16, but the low wages paid to parents "placed great pressure on them to lie about their children's age and to pull them out of school and into the mills at the earliest possible time." The local school board presented no obstacles to this practice, believing that "schools should not interfere with integrating the mill child into the work force."

For this reason school children were given time off from classes so they could bring lunch pails to their relatives already working in the mills, and they often remained to clean and prepare the machines. At the age of 10 or 12, they left school without regret and began to work full time as a sweeper or a bobbin boy. It comes as no surprise, therefore, to find that in 1917 Fall River had the higest illiteracy rate in the United States and that the young children who labored in the mills had only "half the chance of reaching age 20 as the child outside the mills."[3]

Work at an early age for Irish children, legal or otherwise, was not a Massachusetts monopoly. They were employed as early as age seven as "breaker boys" in Pennsylvania coal mines and as newsboys in New York, one of whom, when asked by a well-meaning but intrusive woman why he was not in school, said, "Fait', its little me mudder and daddy cares what I does." At the same time, 1874, and in the same city, mothers sent their daughters onto the streets to sell flowers, a prelude, it was said by the social reformers, to prostitution. More typically, young girls worked at home, assisting their mothers by doing simple sewing or taking care of younger children while their parents worked. In 1853, a Children's Aid Society visitor reported seeing a domestic work arrangement in which "half a dozen Irish girls, sitting in a closet, were making coarse straw bags for a cent a piece." In all such cases, the children did not attend school, and the compulsory education laws, where they existed, were ignored.[4]

Some of the work done by children, in Fall River and elsewhere, was mind numbing. Eddie Dumphy, aged 12, sat on a high stool all day handing thread to another worker for $3 a week, and Gussie Ryan packed stockings in a hosiery factory for 11 hours a day. As an adult looking back, she concluded she had never experienced childhood. By 1911 economic conditions for many Irish families had improved, but even at that date a congressional investigation into the condition of women and child wage earners, found that children's earnings still constituted 65 percent of the total income of an Irish unskilled worker's family and contributed 40 percent to that of a skilled worker.[5]

A similar situation existed among French Canadians in New England. In 1872, in Southbridge, Connecticut, reports of factory accidents included

French Canadian children aged 7–10, and one survey stated that in the Baltic Mills, the town's largest employer, "a large number of children" under age 10 were employed. Massachusetts was ahead of most states in child labor legislation, but statistics for 1891 "showed a higher proportion of French Canadian children at work in the cotton industry in that state than elsewhere in New England." Another study of French Canadians, this time in New Hampshire, found that the family economy was based on the idea that the children would work as soon and as long as possible. One 18-year-old girl who wanted to marry was prevented from going to the altar until her younger sister could go to work.[6]

Available sources seem to show that the Irish used child labor more than the Germans and Scandinavians who came to the United States at the same time. If only urban areas are considered, that was probably true. Many of the immigrants from Northern Europe settled in rural areas, however, where a different kind of child labor was the rule. Farm chores might still permit children to go to school, especially in the winter, but in the other seasons their work was as essential to their parents as the young mill hand was to immigrant parents in a town or city. There were, of course, many differences. Farm children worked directly for their parents, and under normal circumstances would receive better treatment than those who labored for a faceless and exploitive mill owner. Furthermore, farmer's children could look forward to the possibility of inheriting the land on which they labored, and the same could not be said for children working in the mills.

Those youngsters who did become farmers when they grew up had certainly been well trained. From the first moment of settlement on new land in the Midwest, young children "hacked their way through several acres to prepare the soil" for planting. Even more important was the role they played in safeguarding the results of the planting they had done. A Kansas farmwife spoke of her children pulling weeds in the cornfield and described how they "worked as living scarecrows . . . shoving away the whirling birds that threatened to devour the family's future." They also contributed to the family diet by gathering wild plants, especially berries, and by stalking and killing "raccoons, ducks, geese, prairie chickens and, above all, rabbits."[7]

Immigrant farm children, German or Scandinavian, also worked hard at milking cows, feeding chickens, and mucking out the barn. A former farm boy said that "to have to milk two or three cows morning and evening is to be a slave to them . . . but I enjoyed milking, even the cantankerous, tough uddered old shorthorn and the Jersey that kicked like a horse." As was also true for urban children but more so because neither plants nor animals could wait for attention, even very young children were assigned tasks, and school often took second place to household responsibilities.[8]

Later in the nineteenth century, when Eastern and Southern Europeans began to arrive in sizable numbers, they, too, needed their children's wages.

For most Polish families in 1911, the wages of the children of an unskilled father constituted 46 percent of the total family income, 35 percent if the breadwinner was a skilled workman. It seems clear that because one person's "wages were insufficient for even a modest standard of living" for most immigrants, family cooperation was essential. The obverse was also apparent. "The higher the father's wages, the lower the probability of a child's participating in the labor force."[9]

If further evidence of need was required, the fact that in most immigrant families, sometimes under protest, children turned everything they earned over to their parents, keeping only essential carfare for themselves. A 14-year-old Jewish girl's request, for example, to retain a penny to buy candy was refused. She retaliated by refusing to eat dinner, which then provoked a beating with a "twisted towel." A decade or so later such an incident was less likely to occur. By 1920 the sons and daughters of immigrants were beginning to resent "turning over every cent they worked for and having a small allowance handed over to them," and some "simply witheld part of their paychecks."[10]

Children who arrived in America when they were half grown were most likely to accept both the necessity to work and to hand over their wages, because they had done so in Europe. A Russian Jewish woman in Providence, Rhode Island, told an interviewer that she had worked at the family inn, "pouring out drinks and collecting money when she was still too small to reach the counter." Another remembered working as a stock assistant in a Kovno, Lithuania, store when she was 10 years old, and many Italian children had been hired out as farm laborers in Sicily or to work in canneries. A Jewish boy who grew up in Byelorussia was a drayman before he was 13, and his younger brother worked at a nearby grain mill. In Hungary children worked on the family farm as a matter of course, but if the family did not own land they were sent away from home to work as servants or laborers. Uncounted Italian boys were turned over to padrones, who used them in labor gangs all over Europe. Partly for this reason the extension of this system to America, of which more will be said shortly, came as no surprise.[11]

Child labor in the United States, of course, was not exclusive to immigrant children, but it is an important part of their story. This was certainly true for Slovak and Polish families in Pennsylvania. In 1880, although the legal working age was 12, 72,000 children from those ethnic groups, aged 10–15, were working. One girl, Annie Denko, told investigators she had been working in a mill near Scranton since she was 12 and put in 12-hour night shifts, 6:30 P.M. to 6:30 A.M. For girls like Annie, "the mill was her school."[12]

What it came down to was that in many poor immigrant families, if the children did not work because they were too young or otherwise incapable, their mother would have to attempt to supply the needed income. Often this was done by taking in boarders, sometimes by bringing work into the home that could be done by mother and children alike. One Jewish woman in Providence remembered her mother and siblings "bending wire or setting stones" for jewelry. An Italian daughter in the same city said that in her family, "when a child was five or six and could hold a plier," he or she would join the rest of the family around the kitchen table and link jewelry. Photographs taken by Jacob Riis and Lewis Hine show similar scenes in New York's Little Italy, although it was artifical flowers, widely used for women's hats, not jewelry, that absorbed the mother and children's attention.[13]

An account of an ordinary day in an Italian household in 1905 described two small girls working on artificial flowers. "The three year old worked on the petals, her older sister (four years old) separated stems and dipped them in paste while the mother and grandmother placed the petals on the stems." All of this brought 10 cents an hour into the family coffers. Boarders were a nuisance, and home-based work was poorly paid, but many mothers felt it was essential to remain at home. As one woman said, "I have two children and would rather be home to get them something to eat at mealtime." Could no one else do this? Sometimes that was possible. One Italian woman went to work and left her children to be watched by her husband in his barbershop, where, one of the children remembered, "we ran in and out all day long!"[14]

In other situations, relatives were available. Sharing a house in Brooklyn just before World War I, four immigrant sisters-in-law, each of whom had two or more children, took turns taking care of them so that each of the mothers could do piecework in a nearby clothing factory one day a week. Extended family cooperation was the most desirable arrangement in every immigrant community, as it had been for most in their homeland, but in America, the absence of grandparents, maiden aunts, and sisters, at least for the first generation, made child care more difficult. Sometimes, for payment, a neighbor would act as "nanny," and sometimes, especially in Slovak families, a small child would be sent back to grandparents in the homeland.[15]

When all else failed and the need, especially in the absence of a father, was great, a mother might take desperate steps. One interviewee recalled that her mother "eked out the family living" by making aprons, which a son or daughter would peddle on the streets; when an older child's services were not available, her mother tied the small children to the legs of the kitchen table and went out to sell the aprons herself. Day-care centers could have prevented such dangerous situations, but although some existed in New York, at least, there were never enough. In 1917, for example, only 1,400 children, from all the boroughs, could be accommodated. For many reasons, therefore, mothers tried to stay home with their little ones; as a result, older children had to go to work.[16]

According to the 1880 Census, "more than a million children" between 10 and 15 (one out of every six in that age group), were employed. Statistics compiled by the U.S. Immigration Commission, using slightly different para-meters, indicate that 20 years later, the majority of working children were the American-born offspring of foreign-born parents. A slightly earlier survey covering just the state of Illinois came to the same conclusion. One explana-tion for these results was that native-born children of foreign-born parents were better nourished and could read and write English, as opposed to those born into poverty abroad. They were, therefore, more employable.[17]

Foreign-born or American-born, studies of immigrant groups make it clear that most of the children in those communities were at work in their teens, but there were differences in regard to the age at which they entered the workforce. The Immigration Commission survey of seven cities, cited above, found that 30 percent of foreign-born Russian Jewish girls under 16 were at work. American-born daughters, however, were more likely to stay in school a bit longer. Statistics from Boston and the Lower East Side of New York point to 15 as the age that girls born in the United States of immigrant parents entered the workplace. Several other studies based on comparisons between youngsters with immigrant parents and native-born children of native-born parents indicate that this was also true in Providence, Rhode Island. As one would expect, in 1915, two fifths of the latter group were attending high school, and only one tenth of the former, whether born abroad or in the United States, were doing so.[18]

Just as was true earlier in the nineteenth century, when Irish parents were more likely than Germans to use their children's labor, in the later period, Italian youngsters worked earlier and in larger numbers than Jewish children who came to the United States at the same time. The Providence surveys show that in 1915, 95 percent of Italian sons and 78 percent of Italian daughters were working, in contrast to a smaller percentage, 78 per-cent and 58 percent, respectively, of Jewish boys and girls. As these percent-ages indicate, child labor figures for Italians were high, nowhere more so than in Buffalo, New York, where an abundance of canneries provided employment. Even if they were under the legal age of 10, children worked along with their mothers, picking and processing food. Most did this work during the summer, but the Buffalo schools with large Italian enrollments lost 20 percent of their students as soon as good weather made cannery owners signal that workers were needed.[19]

Out of the classroom, into the world, what kind of work did immigrant children do? All kinds. In New York's Five Points, Boston's North End, and in the Irish "Channel" district of New Orleans, children were rag and bone pickers. When Italian immigration was relatively new, in the middle of the nineteenth century, young boys assisted organ-grinders, tending the monkey who accompanied the musician and collecting money from passersby. Later, when the massive influx from southern Italy and Sicily took shape, they were more likely to be newsboys or bootblacks. No group, however, had a monopoly on a specific trade. In Boston's North End, 350 Jewish boys and Italian boys were delivering papers and shining shoes early in the morning and after school.[20]

As the Irish children in Fall River had done earlier, many of the children from Southern and Eastern Europe worked while they were enrolled in school, sometimes in the family store or at home with their mother. Boys carried home bundles of unfinished clothing and delivered articles finished by their sisters to the contractor. Slovene children, some as young as 11, who lived in the Pennsylvania anthracite district also worked after school, cleaning fruit stands, scrubbing meat cases, and, on Saturdays, delivering milk at 3:30 A.M. For most, evasion of school was not difficult. A child might say that he or she was moving to another school district, and the principal would give him or her the papers to present to the new school—at which, of course, the child never appeared. Once out of school for good, Italian and Jewish girls 14 and older embarked on careers in the flourishing New York garment industry, a step up from pulling basting threads and sewing buttons, which they had formerly done at home.[21]

Conditions had not changed much by 1932; in New York's Italian Harlem most working girls did clothing finishing at home, the next largest group worked in dress factories, and only a tiny number did clerical work. Everywhere that a family took in boarders to help pay the rent, immigrant daughters cleaned up after them. Polish boys in Pittsburgh did not work in the large factories until they were about 16; before that age they were newsboys or store clerks or worked in small industrial plants, such as those making glass. In their early teens, Scandinavian boys, especially Finns in Minnesota, might be starting to work in the iron mines, and Slavic boys would do the same in the western Pennsylvania coal mines.[22]

Most of the young workers were exploited, especially the Italians working at the Buffalo canneries and the Greek bootblacks brought to the United States by a padrone. The former group, because they were doing seasonal work that paid very little on a piecework basis, labored from first light, 4:30 A.M., to dark, 10 P.M. Disapproving social workers said that "the little ones old enough to hold a bean are made to work by their parents." One youngster, after a day of snapping beans, said, "my fingers is broke," and the child next to him, who had husked corn for the same number of hours, chimed in with his complaint: the corn silk made him sneeze. Both boys might have had an easier time in a factory but could earn more at the canneries, because there they could do all kinds of work. In the factories, their limited skills made them less valuable.[23]

Looking back, many of the women who had begun to work at an early age remembered their experience as the worst part of their lives. Rose C., who worked as a live-in servant when she was only 14 years old, "slept on two old quilts and a pillow on a bed made of two chairs" and earned $6 a month, which she gave to her mother. Frieda M. recalled the laundry she worked in when she was 12, and said that it was what "you imagine hell is like," because of the lack of ventilation, noise of the machines, and heat.[24]

Lucky enough to be spared such brutal work, but still in need of money, a Brooklyn, New York, boy described an ingenious kind of after-school occupation—errand boy who delivered telephone messages to neighbors who had no phones. "I earned by walking over to the corner drugstore, waiting for the telephone to ring, picking up the receiver and running over to get the person they wanted . . . and was rewarded by a penny or two."[25]

Life was truly hard for working children. Florence Kelley, an activist in the fight against child labor, reported that in an Italian district in Chicago the bootblacks and newsboys went to work at terrible hours and were "ill housed, ill clothed, illiterate and wholly untrained." Even when they worked at home, making artificial flowers, children became ill from the dyes that were used, and those who labored in factories often suffered permanent injuries, such as hernias and spinal dislocations, the fate of some Russian Jewish boys at 13 and 14.[26]

Much child labor was done by boys recruited in their homeland. The padrone system, as it was known in the United States, was an extension of long-standing arrangements in Greece and Italy, where large families and scarce jobs made it necessary for parents to send young boys to places where they could earn some money. In America, the padrone usually made an oral agreement (a written one, if discovered, would lead to punishment for violating the U.S. contract labor law), which among other stipulations required that everything the boy earned, minus deductions for board and room, would be sent home.

Most of the youngsters went to Chicago, far from the sea, which made escape more difficult. Most worked as bootblacks, but some were musician-beggars, such as those who "crowded the streets of Chicago at the turn of the century." Youngsters were often found wandering the streets late at night because they had not earned enough and were afraid to return to their padrone.

Isolated, forced to work from 6 A.M. to 9 P.M., if not longer, beaten if they made requests (to keep their tips, for example), badly housed, and poorly fed, these children, aged 10–12, were a sorry lot. In spite of the fact that most were here illegally, because U.S. immigration law said that children under 16 could not be admitted without a parent, the authorities did little to halt the system. The padrone would claim he was the child's parent and, without a birth certificate, say that his "son" was small for his age, but really over 16.[27]

Trickery of various kinds was part of the child labor process, even when age was not involved. An Italian boy in Lawrence, Massachusetts, got a job as an "oiler boy" at 11 by using his older brother's employment papers, and a Portuguese child in the same city was hired as a dishwasher by a restaurant when he said he was 16. Italians in Providence clothed a daughter in a long dress so she would look older than her years and get work. In his novel *The Jungle,* Upton Sinclair said some of the Lithuanian stockyard workers he was writing about used a false baptismal certificate, stating that their child was two years older than he really was.[28]

Sometimes it was the child who was deceived. Acting on the premise that they could foresee a brighter future for their offspring, parents would force a reluctant child to accept an apprenticeship rather than continue in school. A recently arrived Jewish girl from Galicia came to Philadelphia planning to get an education, but the aunt and uncle with whom she was staying told her that there was "no need to go to school," because in America "every one works." Along the same lines, a Slovene father told his daughter to go to work because she would spend most of her life changing diapers, a task for which schooling was not required.[29]

Jane Addams, one of the activists on the National Child Labor Committee, was primarily concerned with the "children of the foreign born peasant." She was, however, also realistic about his or her family's need for income and was ready to accept the fact that for most such children, their education had to end at age 10. Another progressive, Robert Woods, writing in 1903, also understood that "it was no easy matter for fathers and mothers . . . forever under the galling conditions of precarious employment, to allow a boy or girl capable of adding to the family income," to spend time in school.[30]

Addams spoke from Chicago, Woods from Boston, and a third social service worker, Dorothy Reed, located in New York, reported statistics that bolstered their views. In 1922, the income of an average family in working-class Italian Harlem was $26.98 per week and the rent of an average apartment was $24.23 a month. Clearly, a family with only one wage earner and many mouths to feed, normally the case for Italian immigrants, would need more money. This was equally true for many Jewish families. The Immigration Commission found that in 1911 only 20 percent of Jewish husbands could support their families without help from their wives or children and that in seven major cities 36 percent of Jewish families were dependent on the earnings of their children.[31]

Beyond any doubt, the best way to reduce child labor was to pay adult workers a living wage, but the men and women who wanted to save the children of the poor took a legal approach instead. They were aware that children were hired at cheaper wages than what would be paid to an adult, but they chose to try and keep the youngsters in school and thus off the market for as long as possible rather than support the attempts of the fledgling labor unions for higher wages. Some reformers did approach the problem via the labor movement. One such woman, known as Mother Jones, was an organizer of a 1903 textile workers strike in Kensington, Pennsylvania, when

75,000 workers, 10,000 of them "little kids" aged 10–12, walked off their jobs. Newspaper reports about the strike included a poignant description of the young mill hands: "many had lost their hands, thumbs, fingers below the knuckles and were stooped little things, round shouldered and skinny." Mother Jones was quite skilled at getting publicity, which she demonstrated by leading a march of young workers to President Theodore Roosevelt's estate in Oyster Bay, Long Island, hoping to draw a contrast between the robust health of his children and the sorry condition of the young marchers.[32]

Most of the men and women who wanted to abolish child labor favored a more conventional approach, namely stronger and better-enforced compulsory education laws. Although, as we have seen, there was a law in New York City (then including only Manhattan and the Bronx) requiring children to attend school from ages 8 to 14 as early as the 1880s, it was poorly enforced. This led Florence Kelley, formerly a factory inspector in Illinois and then a coworker of Lillian Wald's at the Henry Street Settlement House in Lower Manhattan, to try to convince residents of the other settlements on the Lower East Side that the child labor problem was a social settlement responsibility. As a result, early in 1902, the Association of Neighborhood Workers appointed a Child Labor Committee to lobby for better compulsory education legislation. The association raised $1,000 and used the money to pay an investigator who discovered more than a thousand violations of the existing child-labor laws.

Partly as a result of this exposé, in 1902 the New York State Legislature passed a law that required children to complete at least the first half of the fifth grade and to reach the age of 14 before leaving school. After a decade had passed, however, the Child Labor Committee began to press for an upward revision of the age and education requirements for working papers, and in 1913 a new law required schooling to age 16 and completion of the sixth grade.[33] Activists in Pennsylvania had succeeded in getting their legislature to pass a more stringent law two years earlier, which required attendance to age 16 and a certificate of literacy before a youngster could be employed. Illinois legislators had accepted the arguments of Jane Addams, Edith Abbott, and Sophinisba Breckenridge and passed a similar compulsory education law at about the same time.

Most of the deception used by parents and children anxious to work was the result of these compulsory education laws. In New York City, for example, many parents could not obey the law passed in 1903 because their children had entered the United States at nine or older and had not been able to overcome their language handicap and complete the fifth grade by the time they reached 14. If employment was essential, working papers were, therefore, procured by illegal means. In response to such laws an angry Italian father in Chicago told an investigator who was looking into his underage child's truancy that there should be a law protecting his rights as well as those of his child.[34]

There can be no doubt that the efforts of the social reformers had considerable effect. The Pennsylvania law cited above, for example, led to a decline of 41,000 child workers. What is also true, however, is that the laws continued to be evaded. Florence Kelley found that in one Italian immigrant colony in Chicago, a large number of bootblacks and newsboys attended school as the law required, but because they had been up since 2:30 A.M., they dozed in the warmth of the schoolroom and learned nothing. Kelley also spoke angrily about the practice of Catholic priests who gave parents a statement saying that their child was two years older than he or she really was, thus permitting the underschooled child to go to work in the stockyards. Kelley's fellow reformers, Abbott and Breckenridge, criticized the principals of schools in immigrant areas for accepting the excuse that a child was needed to stay home and interpret for his parents.[35]

Child labor became much less prevalent after the passage of New Deal labor legislation in the 1930s, but even now, depending on the group, some recently arrived immigrant youngsters are doing what earlier foreign-born children used to do. In one case, the Mexicans, there has been relatively little change. The parents have continued to be migrant farmworkers in California and the Southwest, and their children continue to work alongside them, picking nuts, fruits, and olives. Happily, the number of young Mexicans doing this has diminished, and today it would not be possible to say what was true in the 1920s in regard to one particular kind of work—picking walnuts: "The amount a family could earn at walnut picking depended on the number of children they had and so many were used in the orchards that the schools in their home towns were all but depopulated. Indeed, one closed down completely during the harvest season." In another example reminiscent of an earlier time, a Salvadoran boy, part of one of the newest and poorest groups to arrive in California, works two jobs to support his mother and sisters.[36]

A Chinese girl who grew up in San Francisco in the same decade also remembers having to work, but only during school vacations. Her parents were contractors making denim jeans, and the entire family was taught how to do the work. During the school year, however, there was not much time for the children to help out because after the "American" school day ended they attended classes at a Chinese school from 5 to 8 P.M., and on Saturdays from 9 to 12 A.M. Any leisure time was spent in the shop. As a result, this girl came to believe that "from birth, living and working were inseparable."[37]

What of the transplanted Chinese children of today? A report carrying this title done for the Department of Health, Education, and Welfare (HEW) and published in 1979 showed that 20 percent of those in high school worked after school and 16 percent of younger children did so. Some of the work was done at home, as it had been with the Jews and Italians, perhaps in the very same rooms on Grand Street, Mott Street, or elsewhere on the historic Lower East Side. Others work in the shops and factories that dot the crowded streets of New York's Chinatown.[38]

As a general rule, most students today tend to stay in school even when family incomes are strained. Hispanic youngsters, however, do not. Lydia Vera in Sweetwater, California, for example, left high school and began to work in a fast-food restaurant when her father was unemployed and her mother could not earn enough to support the family. The Vera family's problems were far from unique. "In 1991, Hispanic households earned an average of $22,691, according to the Census Bureau, compared with $30,126 for all households in the United States, prompting many young people to leave school in order to supplement their parent's wages."

There is, however, a difference between this situation and the labor of children of earlier immigrant groups. In the past, they left elementary school early in order to work, but today the 35.3 percent of Hispanics who prematurely ended their education in 1991 dropped out of high school. The difference, however, is not as great an improvement as it seems, because the requirements for white-collar work have moved up with the level of school leaving. In 1893, a child who remained in school to the ninth grade could expect to get a clerical position, something not attainable by a child who leaves from that grade today.[39]

Play

Crowded streets in immigrant areas such as Chinatown are nothing new, but in earlier years they were preferable to even more crowded tenements. Charles Loring Brace, writing about poor Irish children in New York's Sixth Ward, described boys and girls in the milder months living "on the docks and wood piles, enjoying the sun and swimming" instead of remaining in their "wretched tenements." David Nasaw, describing tenement children from various ethnic groups living in various places, agreed that lack of privacy and omnipresent boarders drove youngsters to "roofs, docks, parks (if there were any nearby), stoops and fire escapes." On the streets, they "ran bases, shot dice, tried to hit a ball with a broom handle bat and jumped rope in rhyme."[40]

Many adults also took to the streets and stoops for relaxation and gossip. While the streets were relatively safe from crimes of violence, traffic accidents were not uncommon. Harry Roskolenko, for example, recalled the trauma of his younger sister Esther's death when she was hit by a truck while playing on Cherry Street on the Lower East Side. Poor Esther was only one of many immigrant children killed in street accidents. In 1893, Ettie Pressner, aged seven and recently arrived from Poland found herself in the path of a team of horses on Ludlow Street, also on the Lower East Side, and her nine-year-old sister was unable to save her. Between 1910 and 1913, more than 40 percent of the traffic accidents in New York involved children between the ages of 5 and 10.[41]

Bicycles were also a hazard. Uptown clerks who worked in the financial district of Lower Manhattan would often run into the children who played in their path. One such accident provoked a riot in 1896 when immigrant children and adults, who called the bicyclists "monkeys on wheels," covered the most-used streets with glass, garbage, and sharp stones, pelted the cyclists with eggs and vegetables, and, when business permitted, blocked the streets with their pushcarts. Even when bicycles and trucks were not involved, many of the children's street activities were dangerous. Although they remember it as fun, many youngsters daily risked their lives by running after ambulances and hanging onto horsecars, climbing up to the roofs of their tenement homes, and exploring rat-ridden cellars.[42]

The children playing on the streets took risks rather than acquiesce to parental demands to remain in their jammed apartments. One observer, speaking of Chicago, said "the streets were the true homes of the city's small Italians, Irish and Jews." Certainly they had more room and freedom there and used their free time to play a variety of games, often sex segregated. Little girls played "potsie," which involved drawing boxes on the sidewalk, throwing a marker, and attempting to get to the spot on which it landed on one foot, or they organized games of hide-and-seek or jumped rope in rhyme. Girls and boys played "skully," a poor child's version of marbles, "with bottlecaps filled with melted crayons purloined from school." In general, boys seemed to have greater opportunities for fun and games on the streets. They engaged in a variety of ball games with improvised equipment—stickball with a broom-handle bat, basketball with a ball made of stockings to be thrown against a ledge. Sometimes "real" baseball could be played in a schoolyard or open lot. Although it was much more satisfactory from an athletic point of view, it was often criticized by parents who felt that "running after a leather ball" was ridiculous behavior. Boxball, punchball, and stoopball seemed to draw less criticism.[43]

According to Sophinisba Breckenridge, speaking about conditions in Chicago, most foreign-born mothers did not see the need for play because they themselves were kept busy with assigned tasks from a very early age. Furthermore, they knew that the streets were dangerous, and they did not have time to supervise their children out-of-doors. On the other hand, when hot weather made life unbearable, the streets had an advantage over oven-like apartments, and children were encouraged to play there until a late hour when the air cooled. Parents, of course, also needed relief and stayed up late with them. There were also fire escapes and roofs to use for sleeping on hot nights, but the street was more fun. Day or night, as one author titled his article on the subject "the stoop . . . was the world" for immigrant children and their families, an easy-to-reach escape from their "insect ridden, under-windowed, greasy smelling and porous walled apartments."[44]

It was difficult to find a place to cool off on a hot summer day, but on occasion an ornamental fountain, left over from the days that the Lower East Side was home to the New York gentry, might take the place of a swimming pool. On such a fountain, on Rutgers Street, adventurous boys "would strip and dive into the lowest basin," taking turns watching over "the happily dis-carded pants, shirts, underwear, shoes and stockings." They also took turns keeping an eye out for policemen and, if they saw one, hollered, "cheese it, the cops!" since what they were doing was prohibited by law. Very young children used the sidewalks in front of their house (providing they lived in a front apartment where their mother could look out at them and they could call up for help, if needed). Older ones walked in the neighborhood with boyfriends and girlfriends and, if parents allowed (in Italian families they usually did not), went to local parks or to dances. When family income per-mitted, several children would share a pair of clip-on roller skates, adjustable for many sizes.[45]

In general, there were not many toys in immigrant homes. Dolls, for example, even if they were affordable, were not needed because there was so often a real baby in the household. Some activities, indulged in by both sexes, included climbing mountains of snow created when the streets were cleared, playing in open fire hydrants (if one did not live near a fountain), or swimming in a polluted river, which was both illegal and made children sick. Many of the children who splashed in the East River in New York, for exam-ple, ended up with intestinal disorders and their skin turned "oily brown." Corner and candy stores were favorite "hanging out" places for city boys aged 12 and up, and gambling with cards, dice, or crapshooting was a favorite activity. Movies, where available, were popular, although the films were shown in "dirty, odoriferous, and ill-ventilated firetraps." Although some theaters made young boys and girls sit in separate sections, nature found a way to bring them together, forcing theater owners to hire chaper-ones.[46]

According to the Peoples Institute, whose staff investigated Lower East Side children's leisure-time activities in 1913, "idling" took first place, with baseball a close second. Although it bore the same name as the game Ty Cobb and his teammates played, it was different from the professional sport in a number of ways. With a 5-cent bat (an improvement over the broom-handle) and a 2-cent ball, bareheaded boys organized games in the middle of the street, where most of their running involved escaping from irate store-keepers whose windows were often broken.[47]

Sad to say, city boys in poor neighborhoods also had to run from each other. Gang fights, organized or spontaneous and almost always related to ethnicity, were common. To quote a survivor, Sam Smilowitz, "We had gang fights. Rocks, bottles. Against the Irish. . . . We loaded up the yard with . . . broken bottles that we could throw or use for stabbing . . . we did a job on them . . . the results were a lot of mussed up faces." Gangs were a real problem for many children because their families, seeking lower rents or a few months' concession, would move frequently; the new kid on the block was always a target. The violence described by Smilowitz certainly counteracts a staple of anti-Semitism, the image of the weak and puny Jew. With the same intention, the most famous East Side settlement house, the Educational Alliance, normally concerned with less athletic activities, advocated sports for their young clients.[48]

Perhaps because it was the most foreign city in the United States, New York had the most settlement houses, outnumbering those in other immigrant-receiving cities. The Educational Alliance was only one of several similar New York City organizations. The Lower East Side was also home to the University and Henry Street Settlements, and to Madison and Greenwich Houses, among others. Most were used by children eight years and older, especially girls, but some youngsters would not join their clubs or participate in other activities because they saw them as "too formal, too restrictive and too regulated." For others, such as those who lived on the West Side Italian and Irish district known as Hell's Kitchen, the Hudson Guild was a home away from home to many youngsters, among them author Mario Puzo, who recalled playing Ping-Pong, billiards, and basketball and learning about the theater at the guild, which also sent him and others to a Fresh Air Fund Camp in the country.[49]

The recreational space provided by the settlement houses was extremely important in every big city where open green areas for play were often scarce. Immigrant children whose parents had opted to settle in rural areas, on the other hand, had unlimited access to space, flora, and fauna. "They were great collectors and brought home beetles, snakeskins, fossils, pottery shards, bones, flowers, lizards, and an eclectic variety of animal dung. Some of these items they turned into playthings. A girl built an elaborate doll's house out of buffalo bones . . . and some young Nebraskans took wild melon rinds, turned them inside out, strapped them on their feet and skated around their cabin floor." One farm boy, Charlie O'Kieffe, "referred to flora and fauna almost as people. He ascribed personalities to tumbleweeds and . . . gophers, bobolinks and sand cherries and he remarked on the relative virtues of cowchips and buffalo chips, comparing the latter to matzo and Swedish health bread."[50]

Some cities, where real estate values were low, were able to provide parks because the required acres cost less. The New York City officials, however, were faced with high land prices, especially in the crowded areas where they were most needed. As a result, playgrounds and parks were scarce in the immigrant districts of the city. Jane Addams, after achieving some success in Chicago, went national and organized the Playground Association of America.

Settlement-house workers in all the major centers joined in the fight for parks, which were seen as a means of Americanization and protection from the moral, as well as the physical, hazards of street life. They were willing to start with simple play areas. In Boston, for example, reformers suggested small sandlots, piles of sand bordered by wooden squares large enough to be used by five or six children. The reformers wanted playgrounds "to keep unsupervised youngsters from playing in congested, foul and dangerous streets." They wanted to create a gentler environment for immigrant children, to build parks and playgrounds all over the tenement districts, to provide even a tiny bit of the countryside within the city. They saw playgrounds as places "in which poor immigrant children might learn to play . . . without beating each other up, without gambling, without harassing their elders."[51]

In New York, starting in 1895, various reformers had pressed the city government to level and erect a fence around an unused plot of land in the heart of the Lower East Side. The Outdoor Recreation League raised enough money to equip the area as a playground, and it opened, as Seward Park, in June 1899. Although the city had promised to provide maintenance, it did not keep its commitment. As a result, the park soon became as much of a slum as the blocks around it.

District Superintendent Julia Richman was appalled at conditions in the park, where fagins recruited truant boys for pickpocketing and procurers seduced "bold" girls. Her well-connected fellow directors at the Educational Alliance helped her get to see the parks commissioner to present her plan for making the park safe and useful. She wanted to divide it into "use" areas, one section for girls and older children, one for mothers and young children. Boys were apparently to be barred, and an enclosure shield was to be built around the girls' swings to deter Peeping Toms. She had only minimal success until 1908, when a case of child molestation shocked the community and led the city fathers to make the changes she had suggested.[52]

The current situation in New York City's Chinatown is not much different. Betty Lee Sung, author of the HEW report previously cited, commented on the lack of space for play. Columbus Park, one block square, is the only green space in Chinatown. This tiny area and a few school playgrounds are the only places where Chinese children can safely play. The narrow streets of the district are terribly crowded, and at peak periods of the day they are dangerous. If children were allowed to play freely in Chinatown, the terrible street accidents that occurred on the Lower East Side in earlier years would recur. For this reason, children stay with their working mother after school, and her workplace becomes, in a manner of speaking, their play space, where they can mingle with other children and, if work is slow, play "make believe" in empty cartons. As a result of the limited space for play and the dangers of the streets, some youngsters told Rose Chao, who interviewed them for the HEW project, that they had less freedom in New York than they could remember having in Taiwan or Hong Kong.[53]

Middle-class Chinese children in Queens have more opportunities for play because their parents feel the area is safe and because the city has provided many recreational facilities. Chao found that the larger family income of the Chinese living in Queens meant that toys and bicycles for children were present in almost every home. Furthermore, since fathers did not have to struggle as hard to make a living, they had time to play sandlot baseball with their sons.[54]

From the other side of the continent, a Chinese woman could not recall having had any time to play when she was a child in San Francisco. Every minute of her day was taken up by attending two schools, one the neighborhood public school and the other a Chinese school. During her "extra" time, she worked in the family jeans factory. Playgrounds would have been of little use to her.[55]

Korean girls are also expected to help their mothers because so many married women are in the labor force, but they and their brothers appear to have more time for what Pyong Gap Min calls extracurricular activities. Boys are involved in sports, girls in piano and violin lessons. Boys also take music lessons and girls study art and ballet. Such cultural activities may not be recreational in the usual sense of the word, but neither are they work for monetary rewards.[56] Japanese children are expected to take a share of the family's work, whether on a fruit and vegetable farm near Los Angeles or in a shop their parents may operate. This is in addition to working hard at their studies.

Some of the newest young Asian Americans, the Vietnamese, are also expected to do well in school and help their parents, who have established small businesses in Los Angeles's "Little Saigon." Unfortunately, many have strayed from the paths of school and work into crime. Many young Vietnamese are dropouts, and some belong to criminal gangs. The teenagers do not share the interests of their American peers, possibly because, some community members think, their experience of the war and in refugee camps turned them into delinquents. Perhaps things will be different for their younger siblings.[57]

What emerges from this survey of Asian American children and their leisure-time pursuits is the realization that, much like the children who arrived before them, their opportunities for recreation are limited unless they are part of a middle-class family. There is, however, one important difference. All but the most destitute households boast a television set, an opportunity for passive entertainment that did not exist for the immigrant youngsters of bygone years.

In some ways, the daily lives of immigrant children of the past resembled the lives of many of their American-born peers. As far as working at an early age, for example, their lot was much the same as other children from poor families. It was poverty, not foreignness, that led them to the factory or the dangerous streets. Similarly, all poor children had to use their ingenuity to have fun. Most children growing up in the United States after World War I were less likely to work and more likely to enjoy an increasing number of leisure-time activities. There was, however, one important factor that separated those born abroad or reared by foreign-born parents from those whose roots were firmly established in the United States; the former group had to learn American ways while at the same time working hard and trying to extract as much fun as possible from an often hostile American environment. This is not as true today.

4

Parents and Children

The Immigrant Family

The preceding chapters have presented, directly and indirectly, information about immigrant family values, but more needs to be said on a subject that was crucial to children's lives. In general, Old World values did not produce good relations between foreign-born parents and their native-born children. Foreign-born children who arrived in the United States when they were young also had difficulty accepting their parents' ideas. Differences between the values of the new society and those of the older world from which the parents came, especially when compounded by the pain of leaving everything familiar, the hardships of the crossing, and the difficulties of adjustment, often led to serious family problems.[1]

There can be no doubt that the family was a major factor in the immigrant experience, significant for both the parents and the children of every group. In the late eighteenth century, when many German immigrants came as indentured servants, the possibility that different family members might have to serve different masters was a great concern. Later, immigrant men who came alone saved every penny to bring over their siblings, sometimes their parents, and certainly their wives and children. Some, such as the Chinese who came prior to 1965, were barred by law from doing this, and as a result the "sojourner" communities of Chinese men in New York and San Francisco were very sad places.

For the more fortunate pilgrims who were able to reinstate or create nuclear families in America, marital relationships were not always smooth. Marital unhappiness, anger, jealousy, too many children, not enough money, led to minor and major disturbances. The "poor man's divorce" was not unusual; indeed, the *Jewish Daily Forward* regularly printed columns of names of men who had deserted their families. Alcoholism disrupted many homes, stepmothers were often cruel, and intergenerational conflicts were frequent. In spite of this unhappy litany, however, it seems clear that for many the immigrant family was also a source of strength.

Fate and human failings deprived some immigrant children of this strength. Mothers, exhausted by frequent childbirth and poverty, died young, and fathers were unable to support their children. A Home for Destitute Catholic Children was established in Boston in 1864, and the New York Juvenile Asylum, which sheltered and educated homeless immigrant children, began operations in 1851. Six years later, the German community in New York City established St. Joseph's orphanage at Ninetieth Street and First Avenue.[2]

Other major religious organizations followed suit. Three years after St. Joseph's opened its doors, a German Jewish group, together with the older Sephardic community, established what was to become the Hebrew Orphan Asylum. The young residents were classified as half-orphaned (missing one parent) or entirely orphaned. Boys could remain until they were 13 (maturity for a Jewish male), and girls could stay until they were deemed able to do housework in a respectable Jewish household. The Jewish community was motivated by more than charitable impulses. Had they not created their own haven, they would have stood in danger of losing their orphaned young to another faith.[3]

More fortunate children, whose aunts, uncles, cousins, and grandparents lived within the nuclear household or nearby, grew up with an abundance of family. William Alfred, a member of the fourth generation of an Irish family who first settled in the Cobble Hill area of Brooklyn shortly after the Civil War, described a household that included great-grandparents and grandparents as well as his father and mother. Aunts and uncles were also frequent visitors, something that was true for a Norwegian family in Minnesota as well. In this family, as in many others, the center of attention and authority was the grandmother. One reason for her prominence was that it was often the grandmother who cared for the children when their mother was doing farm work, earning much needed money in a factory, or caring for a younger child. When unmarried adult children came to America without the family matriarch, they created "extra" parents, in the form of aunts and uncles, for immigrant children. Such families, in the "Bloody Ould Sixth" Irish ward in New York City, Carol Groneman said, were tightly woven, as they also appear to be in Betty Smith's autobiographical novel, *A Tree Grows in Brooklyn*.[4]

Sometimes the togetherness could be stifling and lead to rebellion. In any case, it did not encourage individualism. Continuing the pattern of life in their homeland, and feeling vulnerable in their unfamiliar surroundings, most immigrant families emphasized the welfare of the group over that of any specific member. Their own inclinations muted, children in most families were taught to value security over individuality. Italian parents strongly emphasized this value, and some objected to settlement houses because the workers, by teaching children American ways, reduced parental influence. Controlling their young was very important to immigrant parents. Greek children, among others, were raised in "strict obedience and told in clear, blunt language that their principal purpose in life was not to have fun, but to work . . . assume responsibilities . . . and provide for their parents in old age." Family collectivity was very much the rule in Italian and Jewish families in Providence, Rhode Island, among rural Scandinavians in the Midwest, and among Slovaks and Poles in Chicago.[5]

A woman who had grown up in an immigrant family in Providence recalled a cheerful aspect of family cooperation. Her mother and all the children old enough to reach the table worked together making artificial flowers—not, as we have seen, an unusual situation. In this family, however, the collective burden was lightened by sending one child (the one who best understood English) each week to the local movie theater so that he or she could tell the story of the film to the rest of the family and make the time go faster.[6]

Although individual members might have preferred otherwise, traditional family values did not wither away in America, partly because, as in the Old Country, the family group performed important functions. Family economics were as "necessary to industrial capitalism as they (had been) in subsistence agriculture." Thus, "sharing, reciprocity, pooling limited resources and muting individual inclinations" were as essential to survival in the New World as they had been in the Old. There was also an emotional reason for perpetuating close family relations—easing the pain of having severed the ties with the family left behind.[7] Successful conception and birth, for example, were important to immigrant women; as they "separated from their own parental families, children represented the beginning of continuity in America."

To link their present with their remembered past, most immigrant parents prepared ethnic foods, celebrated traditional holidays, and persisted in the religious rituals of their own childhood.[8] Most of the linkage was the responsibility of the mother, and as a result many children who grew up in immigrant families remember their mother as a constant presence in the house and in their lives. If there is one aspect of immigrant family life on which almost all sources agree, it is that the mother was at the center of the household. Although Helena Lopata, writing about Polish Americans, saw a weak mother-child relationship, the opposite seems to be true for most families.[9]

Mothers set the routines and patterns for everyday living and were the source of the limited demonstrable affection and attention available. Unless he or she transgressed in some way, the child of a large family got little parental attention. Much of what parents communicated to their offspring was Old World wisdom, sometimes with a distinct fatalism attached. When Mario Puzo told his mother of his ambition to be a writer and said he would never be happy as a railroad clerk (her ambition for him), she told him, "Never mind being happy. Be glad you're alive." In a similar vein, a Jewish mother might tell a daughter aspiring to higher education and a career to forget her ambition and be grateful to her parents for not pushing her into marriage with a stranger.[10]

Partly as a result of work patterns, in most immigrant families it was the mother who imparted such wisdom because the father was earning a living away from home. Some, especially Greeks and Italians, might be gone for months, working as part of a padrone-recruited gang far from the cities where their wives and children lived; for others, it was simply a 60-hour work week that kept them removed from day-to-day child rearing. A poem by ghetto poet Morris Rosenfeld describes this well:

Ere dawn my labor drives me forth
I have a little boy at home
That seldom do I see
Ere dawn my labor drives me forth
Tis night when I am free
A stranger to my child am I
And strange my child to me

For some fathers, the link to their children was only monetary. If an infant's mother died and there were no relatives to take the child, he or she became a "boarder baby," kept by strangers to whom the father paid "rent." Present or not, however, the father in most immigrant families was the disciplinarian. Mothers might "holler" and administer a slap or two, but it was her words "Wait until Papa comes home" that produced real dread in small hearts.[11]

When Papa arrived, harsh punishment usually followed. To some observers, his liberal use of the "strop" (a piece of leather used to hone a straight-edged razor), his belt, or his hands made him seem uncaring, even brutal, but others saw this behavior as the result of his own upbringing in the Old Country and his experience with his bosses in industrial America. In both cases, unquestioning obedience was the law; breaking that law meant swift punishment. Since it seemed as essential to keep control of his family as it was for him to obey his boss, disobedient immigrant children often felt a heavy paternal hand.

There were still other reasons for the stern discipline. Whatever its long-term benefits, immigration often led to some loss of parental status. It was less acute for mothers, whose nurturing and domestic roles were as important in the new country as they had been in the old, but for fathers, who had looked up to their own fathers as role models who taught them a trade, the inability to do the same for their sons in America may have led them to over-compensate by demanding absolute obedience. Subject to unemployment, periodic or long term, unable to control his own life, a foreign-born father could at least control his children.[12]

One result of this was that immigrant homes were rarely child centered. Children were not praised or exhibited for their cleverness. They were taught to postpone gratification and expected to be obedient, cooperative, and self-reliant. These qualities were demanded from all children, but in Jewish families the approach was somewhat different. The object of Jewish child rearing in many families was to have the youngster "do the appropriate thing at the appropriate time and place." This was accomplished by channeling the child's behavior into work if necessary, school for as long as possible, and religious obligations if the family was observant, all enforced by parental praise and pride. Deviations from this picture of a benevolent, child-centered household were, however, numerous. Memoirs and interviews are full of stories of unhappy children, especially girls, troubled parents (who often turned to the *Forward,* the much-read Yiddish-language newspaper, for advice), and runaways.[13]

Immigrant families often included adolescent children who married young, within a few years of arrival. Although they, like their parents, had experienced an Old World upbringing, their own family values were modified by their American experience, brief though it might have been, as well as by a somewhat better economic position. A strong mother-child bond persisted, and the father was still very much the boss, but he also was more accessible to his children. As a result of somewhat higher income, fathers so inclined could be playful and allow a child, as one daughter remembered, to go through his pockets and keep whatever coins she found. Other men might be able to spare the time and money to take a son to a baseball game. Such options were not available to a father whose first obligation was to keep his offspring alive, but became increasingly likely for his sons and especially his grandsons.[14]

By 1930, Italians, among the poorest members of the 1880–1920 immigrant wave, were no longer as needy, and their family values changed as a result. Evidence accumulated by Caroline Ware in a study of Italian families living in Greenwich Village, New York City, demonstrates this. Men and women less than 35 years old believed that marriages should not be arranged, that large families were not necessarily a blessing, that a husband's authority could be questioned, and that a child should not be required to sacrifice his ambition for the welfare of the family; neither a son nor a daughter owed absolute obedience to their parents. Those over 35 disagreed on all but one of these points, absolute obedience, which they also did not see as important as, for example, arranged marriages.[15]

The family values of a group that has recently become important in American society, Hispanics, resemble those of the Italians who preceded them, probably because they are also Roman Catholic. The father is dominant, male children get preference, the welfare of the nuclear family takes precedence over the wishes of individuals, and members of the extended family play a role in bringing up the children. This is particularly true for the Mexicans who live in the American Southwest and can maintain close contact with the relatives and customs of their homeland.

The mother carries considerable authority, unless, as is often the case, poverty requires her to work long hours outside the home. When both parents are absent, children must fend for themselves. Since they are learning English and their parents probably are not, the family structure is no longer as patriarchal or matriarchal as it once was. Also, as was true for earlier immigrants, when financial pressures are somewhat lifted and American values become more familiar, fathers become less distant and mothers less demanding.[16]

The values of another large and growing group of Spanish-speaking immigrants, those from the Dominican Republic, are much like those of the Mexicans. But according to one observer, there is considerably more pressure on the children to move up the economic ladder. This is not as obvious in Mexican families, but appears to be important to Filipino-Americans, where the father no longer occupies the position of "high priest" but the pressures on children to do well in school and aim for the professions are quite strong.[17]

Much has been said of the family style of the Chinese, the largest of the Asian immigrant groups that have come to the United States since 1965. Many of these studies, such as one by Betty Lee Sung, separate the more recent arrivals from those families formed in the United States or reunited when the Exclusion Act of 1882 was repealed and subsequent laws passed in 1924 and 1952 permitted limited family reunions. The former are the most traditional, the latter, many of whom have reached the middle class, less so. In general, their families are patriarchal, with the father seen as the guardian of Chinese values, including filial piety. For this reason, sons, who will bear responsibility for ancestral graves, are more highly valued than daughters, but all children, regardless of age or sex, are trained to behave as adults.

Anger, self-expression, individualism, and aggression are discouraged, and youngsters are expected to be trouble free, unobtrusive, and quiescent. In one sense, Chinese families are child centered; parents are very much concerned that their children do well in school and, above all, do nothing to bring shame or dishonor on the family. There is, however, little overt affection.

Indeed, a father may exert his authority by keeping an emotional distance from his children. Corporal punishment is rarely used; isolation is more common. Recent studies indicate that longer residence in the United States has brought about some changes in the patterns just described. In general, family discipline is weaker and peer-group pressures on children are much more important. In families that have recently been reunited, the father is a stranger and the mother carries considerable authority.[18]

Japanese have come in smaller numbers, and many are only temporary residents, assigned to the United States by the companies that employ them, but their family values are also of interest. They appear to be similar to those of the Chinese in several ways. Parents are very much concerned with their children. One investigator speaks of "unremitting supervision." Very young children are encouraged to be dependent; their mothers insist that they sleep in the same bed with them. But for older offspring there is little overt affection, an absence of praise, high expectations, and much emphasis on self-discipline and family honor. Like European parents, Japanese immigrant parents living in the United States prior to World War II used corporal punishment and, like the Chinese, isolation to enforce the values they wanted to instill.[19]

Before 1907, there was not much family life for Japanese in the United States, and even when U.S. immigration policy changed, the Japanese-born generation (Issei) knew that they were not likely to move up in American society, but "had high hopes for their American-born (Nisei) children." Indeed, they saw themselves as a "sacrificial generation" and said they stayed in the hostile American society "for the sake of the children." World War II broke down some traditional values, and economic prosperity since the end of the war also had an effect, but even well-to-do suburban families continue to maintain more control over their children than is the case for American society as a whole.

This is especially true in those families who expect to return to Japan. Some of the parents who know that their stay in the United States is temporary send their American-born offspring to Japan for schooling and training while they are still very young. If, however, parental "exile" turns out to be longer than expected, their children come back to live with them, creating many problems for parents and children.[20]

Koreans, who constitute a sizable portion of the "new" Asian immigration, share some of the values of the Japanese and Chinese, such as an emphasis on doing well in school, respect for the elderly, and a willingness to use stiff punishments to instill these attitudes in their young. Recent studies, however, indicate that while older parents continue to be authoritarian, younger ones have adopted much of the American style of child rearing. Least traditional are families headed by the "1.5" generation, Korean born and American raised.[21]

Asian Indian families are among the newest of the new immigrants, and they, too, have high hopes for their children while at the same time maintaining strong control. Their family structure is not as patriarchal, however, partly because fathers are overworked. Other examples, to be discussed later in this chapter, seem to indicate that neither parent is as authoritarian as is the case in other Asian immigrant families and that it is the children who are forcing parents to change.[22]

Marginality

In varying degrees, depending on the group and when they arrived, immigrant children have always been troubled by feelings of marginality. In the "schoolroom they felt foreign . . . at home, they were seen as too American." The "strange dualism" into which they had been born or moved caused much unhappiness for the "little aliens" and their parents. An Italian mother, unable to get her children to obey her command to speak only her native tongue in the house, asked what use there was in having children if she could not speak to them?[23]

Marginality was always a problem, but it seemed to grow more significant as the century of immigration, 1820 to 1920, moved on. Least apparent for German, Irish, and Scandinavian children, it assumed major importance in the lives of Jews, Italians, Poles, and others with Eastern European roots. Perhaps because their numbers were fewer, certainly true for Finns, Danes, Norwegians, and Swedes, perhaps because they looked more like the majority of Americans, the earlier arrivals "melted" more easily. What is certain is that for those immigrant children who came in larger numbers and were seen as more foreign and less welcome, marginality was a central facet of their experience.

A study done in 1936 that asked 600 fifth- and sixth-grade native-born children with foreign-born parents if they felt fully American found that only 15 percent saw themselves in this light. The overwhelming majority said they felt conflicted. The author of the study said that while such children might appear to be assimilated, in reality they were only hyphenated; within them "the old and the new are clearly at war."[24]

This was true of the young men in Jerre Mangione's novel, *Mount Allegro* (1972), who wanted to be like most people but who "realized, as they grew older, that most people were not Sicilians." As a result, they wanted their parents to drop "all their Sicilian ideas and customs and behave like other Americans. Mangione had a particular dread of picnics in public parks (where "spaghetti . . . and wine were consumed with pagan abandon," in contrast to "American families munching neatly cut sandwiches . . . drinking iced tea." Harry Roskolenko, the son of Russian Jews, remembered that outside of the home he saw himself as an American, but to his parents he was only a Jew.[25] Wasyl Halich, who wrote a book about Ukrainians in the United States, would have understood Roskolenko's point well. The dedication in his book expresses much the same feeling: "To American youth of Ukrainian heritage, often living in two environments and between two cultures, not always cognizant of their racial inheritance or their American opportunities, the author dedicates this volume."[26]

Sociologist Pauline Young argued that since immigrant children had to live with their foreign-born parents and thus were certain to receive heavy doses of Old World culture, the best approach to the problem of dualism was for the schools to pay some attention to their ancestral culture. Most educators and social workers did not agree. The former argued that it was their duty to take the children away from evil influences and instill middle-class morality.[27]

Their other goals were to create an intelligent electorate and forge a common American culture. The workers at Hull House, among the most famous of American settlement houses, were very much opposed to bilingual education, especially when taught in an ethnic or parochial school, because they wanted the public school to Americanize immigrant youngsters, who would lead their parents into American life. Some understood why foreign-born parents were distressed by the growing gap between themselves and their children, but, as one of the speakers at a National Education Association conference in 1904 said, the schools must "wrest" these children from their parents no matter what the latter wanted.[28]

Most parents did not agree, and the result of their efforts to keep Old World culture alive when faced with the insistence of the schools that they do otherwise was to create a marginal child, attached by affection and respect to the traditional practices of parents but also eager to be free of some of them. It was a "no-win" situation. When the pressure of Americanized peers and teachers grew too great, children pretended to be other than they were, threw away lunches prepared by their mothers, refused to invite friends to their home, and used many other devices to show how much they wanted to be Americans. One 10-year-old girl, when asked what she planned to be when she grew up, said, "American." Her slightly older brother used one name (American style) when he was out of the house and another (Italian) when he was home.[29]

Children's difficulties hurt their parents, themselves torn by the desires to preserve their native culture and to see their children get ahead in the New World. As one Polish father said, "it is Mary or Stanislaus (his children) who must talk to the gas man, the insurance man and the doctor in the hospital," thus diminishing his stature in the household. This parent, like many others, when unable to solve a problem relating to American society, fell back on proverbs taught to him by his grandfather rather then say "I don't know." The most insistent of the Americanizers, when told of such painful occurences in immigrant households, argued that it was the father's responsibility to learn English, read the newspapers, and thus cross over to the American side to join his children. Given the economic realities, however, this was not an easy assignment, even for parents willing to do so.[30]

And most were not—indeed, some immigrant parents, feeling devalued in the New World, exaggerated the power and glory of the their homeland. Another Polish father found himself in an embarrassing situation when his daughter, whose head he had filled with stories of Poland's greatness, discovered that her father's native land had been carved up like a Thanksgiving turkey at the end of the eighteenth century. More damaging than this fact was her realization that she could not trust him to tell her the truth.[31]

Other immigrant children hurt their parents by trying to keep them away from school. Shirley K. remembered that she and her friends were careful not to give their teachers a reason to call for their parents, because the prospect of a shawled woman, speaking broken English to their "white gloved, hatted lady teacher," was too much to bear. Mothers were often aware of this and avoided parent-teacher meetings or any other kind of exposure to their children's world. Some tried to follow the path recommended by the Americanizers and, especially if there was an older daughter in the house to clear up after supper and see that the younger children went to bed, did try to learn English in night school. The same Shirley K. who was ashamed of her mother also remembered her efforts to learn the English alphabet and to read an English newspaper. Unfortunately, tired from the work of raising four children on a minimum income, it was a struggle she could not win.[32]

Some parent-child public activities could not be avoided and caused much pain. Jerre Mangione recalled his anguish when his mother, to whom bargaining was the customary way to shop, wrangled with a salesman in broken English over the price of a pair of trousers she was buying for him. Another Italian, John Fante, felt the same way when his grandmother tried to speak English to his friends. Fante acted out his hostility by denying that the man whose name he bore was really his father. Samuel Ornitz hated his mother for calling him "ziegelle" (little goat), which to her was a term of endearment but to him a source of humiliation.[33]

Name changes, sometimes prompted by the children themselves and sometimes by the outer world's inability to pronounce foreign names, were a source of difficulty for parents and children. Leonard Covello recalled his father's fury when he discovered that a teacher had taken it upon herself to remove the "i" that was part of his name (Coviello). "What has this Mrs. Cutter have to do with my name?" he thundered. His wife entered the fray, trying to make peace by assuring her husband that it was a mistake that would be rectified, but Leonardo, wanting to keep his Americanized name, kept saying, "You just don't understand, you just don't understand."[34]

Many teachers took a step similar to the one that so enraged Covello's father, but usually it was the first name that was changed. Giovanna became Jenny, Dominica became Minnie, Giovanni and Guiseppe became John and Joe. Jewish children were also renamed at a teacher's suggestion. "Paia became Pauline, Devorah, Dora, Rivke emerged as Ruth or Rachele, and only Naomi refused to become an all too Irish, Nellie."[35]

It was partly the mispronunciation of her name (Pavlova instead of the correct Pawlowska) that led one young Polish immigrant girl to give up on her public school and transfer to a heavily Polish parochial school, where there were many Polish teachers and "surnames were not mangled." She was much happier there. Similar feelings were expressed by Thomas Napierowski, who attended a heavily Polish parochial school that reinforced his identity and minimized potential conflicts between his family and the larger American society. He also credits the solidly Polish enclave in which he grew up for this. Other children were less fortunate. Rosemary Prosen lived in an equally closed-off Slovenian enclave in Cleveland, but drew no support from her neighborhood. When a boy in ninth grade told her that she "talked funny," she spent a precious 25 cents on a pamphlet that provided pronunciation exercises and then practiced secretly in the bathroom, especially the troublesome "th" sound.[36]

Place of birth and age on arrival had much to do with an immigrant child's feelings of marginality. A woman who had been born in Russia and came to the United States at age six remembered the poverty and hardships that had led her parents to uproot themselves and "understood that they did this for their children." As a result, she appreciated the advantages of growing up in America and tolerated her parents' foreign ways. Her younger sister, however, rebelled against Old World strictures. Born in America, she was ashamed of her mother, father, and an older sister who was born in Europe, was too old for school, and was therefore sent to work in a garment factory. Others did not openly rebel but were never comfortable. Some felt that they didn't belong anywhere, some that they lived in two worlds, "too foreign for the schoolroom, too American for their home." Marginality had a bad effect on immigrant children, making them feel insecure and rejected and causing intergenerational hostility.[37]

The study of the human psyche, child and adult, has come a long way since the years in which European immigration was at its peak. Do the Asian and Hispanic children who have come to the United States more recently also experience a feeling of marginality? With a few exceptions, yes. A third-generation Japanese-American girl who grew up amidst Japanese culture felt very much at home with it at the same time that she was doing well at

UCLA, but the same article that described her adjustment said that most of the Sansei (third generation) rejected the patterns followed by their parents and grandparents.[38]

This did not, however, solve their problems. As late as 1975, teachers singled them out and Americanized their names. One ignored the real name of a Japanese American student and called her May because that was the month of her birth, and when another instructor used her proper name, Kyoka, her classmates called her "Cocoamalt." Her reaction was to turn away from the children of her own ethnic group, who spoke to each other in Japanese, and to criticize her parents, who observed traditional amenities with neighbors and friends. Above all she yearned to be lighter skinned, tall, and long-legged. The extent of her self-hatred seems extreme and unrealistic, but in one regard she fits into the same pattern followed by immigrant children of earlier groups, that is, she envied her peers who had Americanized parents.[39]

A close observer of Japanese teenagers at a Sacramento, California, high school said that they were troubled and conflicted about their ethnic identity. They asked, as had many immigrant children before them, "Are we Japanese Americans or Americans of Japanese ancestry?" Many decided to break away from the shy, submissive, and docile stereotype "that accompanied either description and chose to be called Asian Americans and wanted to be seen as people who would stand up for their rights."[40]

A Filipino American girl whose parents did not go to school functions had a different reaction. Fearing that their inability to speak English would make others laugh at them and shame her, she was relieved at their lack of interest. The children of the newest Asian Americans, those from Vietnam, have been taught to speak their parents' language and do speak it at home, but, as one girl said, they are only "transitional Vietnamese because they think in English and are more comfortable in that language." Furthermore, those who have become "fluent in English no longer communicate easily with their parents, who are comfortable only in Vietnamese."[41]

Youngsters who have made a commitment to the American way have undoubtedly made their parents unhappy, but are probably better off than some, such as Chinese American children, who continue to accept dual messages. Sociologist Betty Lee Sung noted a number of conflicts between accepted behavior in their own homes and the ways of the American mainstream. These include the absence of overt affection from their parents versus the expressions of love they see among their peers, thrift as opposed to conspicuous consumption, avoidance of aggressive behavior rather than "macho" behavior, and respect for authority as opposed to back talk.[42]

Maxine Hong Kingston described a dreadful example of how Chinese custom can conflict with American classroom expectations. Her mother, in accordance with Chinese custom, had cut her overly tight frenum (part of her tongue) when she was born, under the impression that it would give her daughter the freedom to speak in many languages. The result, however, was to inhibit her child's ability to speak English, and because of this she "flunked" kindergarten. So did other Chinese children, who had been taught that to be quiet was a virtue.

Kingston, who was later successful as a teacher and writer, seems to have had a particularly difficult time growing up Chinese American. Her mother forced her to ask the local pharmacist, who was a Caucasian, for candy to remove the curse he had placed on her household by attempting to deliver unordered medicine. Trying to explain this Chinese custom to the drugstore proprietor was torture, but preferable to other cleansing actions her mother was prepared to take. Truly, "understanding neither the Chinese culture of her immigrant parents nor the American culture of her school and neighborhood, she was bewildered and intimidated by both."[43]

Fifty-one Chinese families settled in Mississippi around 1870 to work as sharecroppers, and enough of them remained 100 years later to form a community of 1,200. Their children had an enormously difficult experience because their Old World culture was denigrated and because they were not white. The majority society of the Mississippi Delta recognized that they were not black either but, afraid to offer equality to people of any color but white, treated them unfairly. The Chinese response was to adopt, as much as they could, the majority's language, culture, and behavior. To an extent that would have delighted advocates of assimilation in the North, the Delta Chinese tried to be seen as white. Today, many of their children, although they may feel guilty, "do not want to take part in all-Chinese events." Those who do attend "also express ambivalence about their participation and their Chinese heritage." One young adult told an interviewer, "I don't fool with the Chinese at all." Non-Mississippi Chinese, less Americanized, call such people bananas, "Yellow on the outside, white on the inside."[44]

Younger Russian Jewish immigrants are adopting American ways quickly. "When asked if they consider themselves Russian or American, almost all of the young children will answer American without a moment's hesitation. Few remember much about the country of their birth; Brighton (the Brooklyn district that has become a center of Russian Jewish settlement) is the only home they know. Although they speak Russian at home, most speak English to each other, replete with all the latest Brooklyn slang. And, like American-born youngsters, they dress in jeans, T-shirts, baseball jackets, and stylishly cut sweaters and sneakers."[45]

Their older siblings are having a harder time. As is true of most teens born abroad, they find it difficult to fit in with their American peers. "As confused about their parent's identity as they are about their own, many Russian teenagers have a very difficult time finding out what place they want to occupy in American society." As one said, "It is hard to know what we are supposed to be becoming." Difficult, certainly, but it appears that the current group of Russian immigrants has been spared one unpleasant aspect of becoming American, conflict with parents. Persecution and hardship under the Soviet regime have made most of the emigrés ready to accept Americanization.[46]

Intergenerational Conflict

In most cases, this was not true for those who preceded the Russians. Numerous autobiographies and memoirs attest to the stressful relationships that became a part of growing up American in a family in which parents wanted children to retain Old World culture and traditions. As Marcus Hansen said, there was a huge gap between the children and their parents, difficult to bridge and productive of conflict. Some parents, aware of the divide, tried to close it via ethnic schools, and when the children went along, the estrangement was limited. Indeed, some youngsters rebelled against Americanization and wanted to know more about the "world of their fathers and mothers." It was more likely, however, that a child feeling the pain of marginality would choose to reject the Old World culture of parents. As Oscar Handlin said, "it was very difficult for the old timers to show their children the right way around the twisting curves of the new way of life."[47]

The potential for intergenerational conflict is of course present in every family, but exacerbated when parents are foreign-born and children are not. The topic most discussed (after poverty) in the records of the San Francisco Italian Welfare Agency was "the friction between immigrants and their children." An observer in New York City said that "the lack of understanding between young Italian girls and their parents [and their] lack of confidence . . . is pictured again and again in the scenes of the courtroom."[48]

Other ethnic groups did not avoid the problem, unless, as was true for those who settled in a small and homogeneous community, the process of Americanization was slow and the young were educated in Old World traditions. Unlike the child who lived, as we have seen, in a border world, neither American nor foreign, parents and children in smaller communities seemed to avoid the cultural dislocation so marked in large cities. But not entirely. Finnish families who settled in mining communities in northwestern states said that "in the morning as the children go off to school, they still speak Finnish; in the evening, when they return, it has been forgotten." This was much regretted by their parents. As one contemporary article said, "Can you feel the heartache of a mother as she sees the child slip away into another world? Thither she cannot follow for she has not the key."[49]

In the urban ghettoes, it was common for children to try and convince their parents to adopt American ways by telling them over and over again that they were in a new land where Old World ways were inappropriate. This only "increased parental insecurity about what was right for their children," which sometimes was translated into harsher measures to control them. Parental discipline, however, was not easy to enforce in the New World because, among other reasons, it was more difficult for fathers and mothers to show their children their talents and strengths. In Sicilian villages and in the shtetels of Poland, children could see the nature and results of their father's labor, but in New York or Chicago, where he was likely to do rote work in a factory his children never saw, his authority was diminished.[50]

As we have seen, a major bone of contention was parental insistence that whatever a child earned be turned over to his or her parents. Although the money was often needed, the demand was also a way to compensate for lack of control. The amounts were not insignificant. In the early years of the twentieth century, a Slovenian girl who earned $13 a week was allowed to keep 50 cents, and her younger siblings, who brought home less, got to keep only a few cents.[51]

In many families, children and parents understood neither each other's words nor the meanings behind them. Some mothers and fathers, although they might understand a little English, insisted on using only their native tongue at home and became hurt and angry when answered in a language they could not understand. Even when the children knew some Italian or Yiddish and were willing to use it, the content of their words was foreign to their parents' ears. Telling your mother that she was not following American habits of personal cleanliness, such as daily baths and frequent brushing of teeth, even when said in perfect Polish, was not likely to produce harmonious family relationships.

Even the children willing to speak their parents' language at home did not want to be identified as foreign when in public. A Jewish youngster remembered riding an El train and moving far away from his mother because he did not want to be seen sitting next to a person reading the Yiddish paper. One aspect of the language quarrel, however, was useful to the heads of the household. When their children refused to learn or use their parents' language, mothers and fathers were able to exchange ideas and make decisions without their offspring knowing what they were saying. Even when the parents knew English, they often used Italian or Yiddish or Polish when they wanted privacy.[52]

Hygienic information came from the schools, which made it difficult for parents to ignore. It was, however, easier to keep their children isolated after school hours by making stern rules about when they could leave the neighborhood and with whom they could play. "We cannot have any control over him when he is out of the neighborhood," was the view of many immigrant parents. Sometimes the policy backfired. One youngster told a social worker who had asked him why he missed so many classes that he did it because it was the only time he could go downtown. "I know that my parents would not let me go otherwise."[53]

Getting away from the house was a persistent issue. An interested observer of Lower East Side family life when Russian and Polish Jewish immigration was at its height said that many a boy ran away "from the supper table to join his gang on the Bowery where his talent for caricature was developed at the expense of his parents." Often the runaway did not go far. Mario Puzo's refuge was a perch overlooking the New York Central railroad tracks adjacent to his house. For Harry Roskolenko the East River brought solace.[54]

In such cases, although parents knew where their children were, they raised strong objections to their idleness. "She loathed idleness . . . to her laziness was just sitting unless your hands were busy," said one woman of her Slovene mother. She illustrated the point by specifying the tasks her parents assigned to her and her siblings. Most of them were basic: fetch water, empty slops, clean the privy, etc., and if a girl child wanted to do something more creative, such as cooking, Mama sensed a rival and said no. This, in turn, might lead a girl to reject her mother's "old-fashioned ideas." Such ideas, when applied to clothing, were even more bitterly contested. Most immigrant mothers favored utilitarian, durable garments and paid little attention to style, but to Americanized daughters, preteen and a bit older, style was of the greatest importance. When family income permitted, battles raged.[55]

Girls were generally seen as a greater problem than boys to immigrant parents. One mother said that she had six children, three boys and three burdens! A father, when presented with a fourth daughter, told his family and friends, "It's just another girl." The reason behind these negative attitudes was not sexism per se but rather the belief that daughters were a greater responsibility. They needed more protection, husbands (who would probably insist on a dowry) had to be found for them, and, because women were paid less, they were less likely than a son to earn their keep.[56]

Young girls responded to these attitudes in various ways. Most liked the idea of an early marriage because it was a chance to get out of their parents' house and manage one of their own. Others, less eager to exchange parental domination for a husband's rules, might insist on marrying later but, in the long run, acquiesced in parental decisions. There were certainly exceptions, but until fairly recently it took considerable courage for a girl to opt for "spinsterhood" and live independently. For this reason, most of the girls in foreign-born families married early to a man approved by their parents.[57]

Even when they generally obeyed a father's or mother's "diktats," American-born or -raised children were perceived as arrogant and disrespectful when they questioned Old World authoritarianism. In addition, the children's aspirations often seemed ridiculous to parents. When Harry

Roskolenko's mother heard that he wanted to write poetry, she scoffed, "A poet you want to be? With what—with your foolishness?" Roskolenko's response to his mother's put-down, exacerbated by bitter quarrels with his father over another issue that drove parents and children apart—religious observance—led him to run off to sea at an early age.[57]

Most, however, stayed with their family until marriage, but not without considerable conflict. Some mothers were skilled conciliators, their talents honed to perfection by years of trying to keep the peace, but sometimes even their best efforts failed. When a son criticized the decor at home for being too Italian, his father beat him. This was also the fate of a daughter in another family who came home later than the hour her father had specified. One young girl attempted to wear lipstick at age 13, which brought about a harsh scrubbing from her mother. Resentment at such treatment sometimes escalated into crisis; even if their youth and poverty forced them to stay at home, immigrant children left their parents in terms of culture, behavior, and affection.[58]

The worst-case scenarios were played out in the years before World War II, but families coming to the United States in more recent years have not entirely escaped such problems. There are, however, considerable differences in the way the newest immigrants have dealt with intergenerational conflicts. If there is much parent-child conflict in Chinese American families, for example, it is well hidden. Three recent investigations have nothing to say on the subject, although Rose Chao's report, completed in 1985, said that it is to be expected, because, increasingly, American-born Chinese peers are providing the counseling and direction that immigrant parents cannot. Recent examples of antisocial behavior among Chinese youth, to be described later, seem to show that Chao's forecast was accurate. Another source, however, says that whatever disharmony does exist is based on communication difficulties, not substantive issues.[59]

Japanese American families also seem to avoid conflict, although members of the generation born before World War II recall feeling resentful when they had to attend Japanese school after going to public school and doing household chores. Such feelings, however, rarely came out in the open because, in general, Nisei children found it difficult to disagree with their fathers. It was apparently somewhat easier for children to be more willful when Japanese families were in internment camps, where parental authority was greatly eroded.[60]

A third group of Asian immigrants, Koreans, do experience intergenerational problems if the parents are somewhat older, but not in families formed in the United States. Disagreements in Southeast Asian Indian families, also not very pronounced, are in some cases settled in favor of the children. A study done in 1980 said that Indian parents adapted to fast food in deference to their children's wishes and have accepted "other changes in the pragmatic aspects of life . . . but have strongly resisted alterations in their core values." The result has been "a widening of the generation gap and . . . value conflict."[61]

Family differences have caused problems for another group of immigrants from the Asian subcontinent, Bangladesh. Parents of this group have found that their children have no interest in continuing the cultural and religious practices of their parents because, unlike their elders, they have no desire to return. Increasingly, parental requests to remember their heritage— to "speak Bengali at home and, if Muslim, pray five times a day, refrain from eating pork or sipping alcohoic drinks"—fall on deaf ears.[62]

For both Indian and Bangladeshi parents, teenage dating is a major source of conflict. This is even more the case for the one European group, Jewish emigrés from the former Soviet Union, that has arrived in recent years. Because "the reality and conception of adolescence" was very different there, parents transplanted here do not understand how difficult it is for their offspring "to learn English quickly in order to do well in school and to fit in socially." Parents are also "shocked by the relative laxness and freedom of the New York City schools and of American culture in general." In the old USSR, adolescent children were much more restricted by their parents and the institutions of Soviet life. Drugs and sexual experimentation were not part of teenage life, and organizational activities sponsored by the state were important. Ethnic identification, such as being Jewish, was not significant in Moscow or Odessa, but in New York it is, contributing to the "identity confusion" of both immigrant children and parents.[63]

Haitian children also feel pressured by conflicting forces, but their disagreements with their parents center around the same issue present in the Bangladeshi community: is their stay in the United States permanent or will they be required to return to their parent's homeland? Most want to stay here, and as long as poverty and repression continue to exist in Haiti, the matter of return is moot.[64]

The intergenerational conflicts of a different group of people from the Caribbean, Cubans, are more like those of the European immigrants who preceded them. Two factors—parental insistence that family needs take precedence over individual desires and a wish to be more American than Cuban—have plagued Cuban American families for 25 years. A recent study concluded that "Cuban adolescents tend to be more Americanized while Cuban parents tend to adhere more closely to their Cuban roots. The parents become alienated from their . . . Americanized children [who] in turn experience alienation from less acculturated parents." The passage of time, however, has also produced some positive results. Gradually, as their sons and daughters become more and more acculturated (and learn how to drive), the new idea of greater independence for children has been accepted by more progressive parents, who by 1980 were able to say that much of their knowledge of the "correct American way, came from their children."[65]

Delinquency

This positive development may spare Cuban parents and the community they live in from some of the worst results of intergenerational conflict, such as delinquent behavior on the part of their young people. This had not been the case for earlier groups. Family divisions, of course, were not the only reason Irish, Italian, and Jewish children, among others, became enmeshed in the criminal justice system, but most observers believe it was an important factor. The standard work on Poles, for example, says that the children of immigrants were "demoralized," that is, had lost the moral principles of their parents because they had lost respect for them. This, in turn, led to vagrancy and dishonesty among the sons and sexual misbehavior among the daughters.[66]

In 1850, half of the children in reformatories and houses of refuge in New York City were either immigrants or the children of immigrants. Three years later, 50 percent of the troubled children sent to the West by the Children's Aid Society were also "little aliens" or the native-born offspring of foreign-born parents. Children's Aid workers, like the Progressives later in the century, were environmentalists who blamed the conditions under which the Irish and German immigrant children lived for their delinquency. Visitors described filth, "reeking hallways," crowded rooms, drunken fathers, beaten mothers, and terrible poverty in the Irish Five Points tenements. They sorrowfully said that with enough time and money the Children's Aid "could have made a wonderful man" by removing a boy growing up in such circumstances, but because the resources were not available, he would grow up and become a criminal. Then, they said, "we can only hang him."[67]

In their first annual report, in 1854, the Children's Aid Society was specific about the crimes committed by Irish immigrant children. Picking pockets was a well-organized "profession," complete with "decoys" and "coverers" to entice victims and protect the thieves if they were caught. There were also "feelers . . . to ascertain where . . . depredation could be most easily committed." Some of these areas were the wharves, where cargo could be stolen and then resold and where new arrivals could be robbed.

For delinquents girls, the streets provided customers for prostitution and sometimes opportunities for theft as well. Children's Aid reports indicate that juvenile delinquency was present everywhere in Lower Manhattan, but to a lesser degree in areas where German immigrants predominated. On the other hand, in a very poor German area on the far East Side around the foot of Forty-second Street, the Children's Aid Society found many juvenile lawbreakers. It also targeted the Italian section of the Sixth Ward, farther downtown on the East Side, as a troubled district with many actual and potential young criminals.[68]

Most children born to Irish immigrant parents, whether in Ireland or in the United States, did not run afoul of the law, but their remembrances provide reason to believe that they may have had a narrow escape. They seem to have received little overt affection and to have grown up in an atmosphere rife with fatalism and superstition. Imprudent praise of a child, it was said, could alert the "evil eye" and bring the devil's attention to the child who was commended. Children were treated as children, "not small adults," and as a result, they learned "to be subordinate, obedient, respectful and polite. Punishment was always at the ready."[69]

Such treatment was typical in other immigrant families. A second-generation Norwegian son, for example, said that his father remembered his own parents as severe disciplinarians."[70] This was also true for others. An Italian father locked his children out of the apartment if they were late for meals, and social workers commented unfavorably on the "spanking, cuffing, punching and slapping" that went on in Slavic and Italian households. One Jewish woman remembered that her father tried to teach her the alphabet at the same time that he punished her. If she was untidy and failed to clean up her room as expected, his procedure was to administer a blow for each letter of the appropriate word: S (slap), L (slap), O (slap), P (slap), P (slap), Y (slap)—*sloppy*.[71]

Harsh punishments, deserved or not, certainly provided children with reason to rebel, but contemporary scholars speculating on the causes of delinquency among immigrant children have suggested that parents' inability to orient themselves to American life led their sons and daughters to look for support elsewhere. Some found it from teachers or religious leaders, but many children obtained guidance from other children by joining a gang. As one examiner of the Italian American family put it, "Italian youngsters identified with their peers, rather than with their parents."[72]

Virginia Yans-McLaughlin, writing about Italians in Buffalo, said that antisocial behavior was limited, but where it did exist, it was the result of the Italian family's inability to help children to adjust to American life. The children, confused, sought clarification from their peers, sometimes as part of a gang. Thomas Churchill and Joseph Hawes agree with this analysis, citing the two sets of values to which many immigrant children, Italian or otherwise, were exposed. Hawes also found that "children of immigrants were more likely to become juvenile delinquents" because they were poor, and poor people are usually more attracted to crime. Many of the youngsters picked up by the police, who, in general, were hard on "slum kids," began their careers as junkies, sorting through refuse for anything of value that they might sell, and then moved on to become thieves.[73]

Confusion as to who they were, however, was not the only reason immigrant children turned to delinquency. Indeed, some parental attitudes, often brought from the Old World, led directly to antisocial behavior. To survive growing up in poverty and oppression in a Sicilian village or in a shtetel in the Russian Pale often meant unorthodox and illegal behavior. Especially in the early years of settlement, some of the same means might be useful in America.

In any case, there were certainly a variety of reasons to explain why immigrant children became delinquents. As we have seen, poverty and the belief in family collectivity led immigrant parents to take all of their children's legitimate earnings, which in many cases led their resentful offspring to find sources of illegitimate funds. Sometimes this led a child to run away and become a thief in order to live, and sometimes stealing was done for more noble purposes. One boy who was forced to give all of his wages to his father stole some cheap jewelry at Christmastime to give to his little sisters, who were not likely to get gifts from their impoverished parents. Joseph Hawes, who told this poignant story, was writing about Chicago, where in the 1890s most of the juveniles arrested were the children of immigrants and where 70 percent of the children coming before the juvenile court had foreign-born parents.[74]

Jewish children were not immune to delinquent behavior. As late as 1935, 58 percent of New York City's juvenile criminals lived on the Lower East Side, representing an increase from 1927. This was in spite of the fact that the Jewish population of the Lower East Side as a whole had declined in those years. Perhaps borrowing from the Irish pickpockets who operated earlier in the nineteenth century, Jewish "grifters" also worked in pairs; one distracted the "mark," while the other stole the gentleman's watch or the lady's purse. They were often caught; in 1906, 28–30 percent of all the children brought to Children's Court were Jews, most of whom had recently arrived in the United States. The percentage decreased in the following years. Data from 1911 and later indicated that more than 18 percent of the juvenile arraignments in Children's Court were of Jewish children and that most had not been arrested for serious offenses but for peddling illegally or running away.[75]

Mario Puzo, in New York, did not belong to a gang, but he certainly was a delinquent, stealing ice from the railroad refrigerator cars in the summer and coal from open carriers in the winter. Polish children did the same thing in other cities. Some were caught and brought before a judge. In the decade 1910–20, 72.8 percent of the 14,183 children who were tried in the Cook County (Chicago) Juvenile Court had foreign-born parents. Those who had committed serious crimes would probably be sent to reformatories, to the relief, according to one observer, of their parents.[76]

Youthful criminality was least likely in rural areas, where the process of Americanization was slow, young people were more likely to accept Old World traditions, and there was little cultural dislocation. There was also less to steal and fewer ways to spend money, all of which encouraged law-abiding behavior. Every immigrant group, past and present, who settled in urban centers, except recent arrivals from India, seems to have problems with delinquent children. The Chinese community in recent years has been plagued by youth gangs. Their activities include extortion, robbery, and murder. According to Betty Lee Sung, they are "almost without exception composed of immigrant youths, many of whom cannot keep up their school work."[77] Mexicans in Los Angeles have similar problems. School dropouts, unable to find work, turn to their peers and start down a path that leads to prison. The Dominican community in New York is riddled with drug dealers, many of them barely in their teens, and conditions are not much better in "Little Havana," Florida.[78]

If the past is any indication, some of this will decline with legitimate economic success. This was certainly true for the Jews, whose youthful delinquents grew up to be well represented in organized crime in the interwar years but, when able to achieve success by more respectable means, left violent crime behind.

In some respects, when one is aware of the extent of family breakup and consequent damage to children today, the immigrant family of the past appears to be a model of strength and stability. Single-parent households, of course, were not unknown in immigrant communities, and some intergenerational conflict is built into parent-child relationships wherever families exist. What does seem to have changed, however, is the fact that the problems seem to have become more pervasive, or at least more publicized. Family breakup in middle-class American families now appears to be more of a problem than it was for the immigrant poor, and juvenile delinquency appears to be much more widespread. Marginality, however, that very troublesome aspect of the immigrant child's experience, may be less of a problem today, when children are taught to respect ethnic differences. Time will tell if this is to be the case.

5

Summing Up

Whatever the long-term benefits, growing up American is not a smooth or easy process. The boys and girls who make the transoceanic journey with their family or are born to immigrant parents in the United States have many difficulties to overcome. As we have seen, their problems have varied with their place of origin, time of arrival, and destination. In spite of some dissimilarities, however, they had much in common. There was a vast difference between the trip a Polish child took to America in 1880 and the one a Chinese youngster took a century later, but the experience was traumatic for both. Unless they were infants in their mother's arms, they were leaving behind the familiar for the unknown and facing an uncertain welcome, vulnerable to "the slings and arrows" fortune held in store. The process of leaving the Old Country and entering the New changed with the years, but the feelings engendered remained much the same.

What has also remained the same is the role children play in the process of acculturation, a central part of the immigrant experience. To a great extent, children are translators and interpreters, bringing home messages from the larger society. An English-speaking child, even one quite young, is of inestimable value to parents, especially mothers, buried at home with the burdens of raising a large family on a small income. Thanks to the children, information on health care, manners, proper dress, and food preparation, although not always welcome, penetrates the immigrant household and accelerates the melding of old and new. American children, as they mature, can often be mediators between their foreign-born parents and the outside world, a pipeline for American ideas.

With some exceptions, poverty was and is omnipresent in the settling process of every immigrant group. For many, it lasts for a long time. Inadequate income has colored every aspect of children's lives, whether the offspring of Irish peasants fleeing exploitation and famine, of Italians from Sicily unable to feed their children, of Russian Jews victimized by the economic effects of discrimination, or of Mexicans migrating for survival. Lack of money determined the conditions of daily life as well as the future prospects of all the immigrant children arriving before World War I. To a somewhat lesser degree, poverty plays a central role in the lives of Mexicans, Dominicans, Vietnamese, and Haitians today.

Overlooking for the moment the physical aspects of their lives, such as terrible housing and skimpy meals, it is clear that limited schooling and work at an early age were the most damaging results of the pervasive poverty that was the condition of most immigrant families. There are, of course, considerable differences of degree and kind. The groups that came the earliest, such as the Irish, were the poorest, while some, such as the German Jewish refugees of the 1930s, brought resources, tangible and intellectual, that allowed them to escape dire poverty. Many of those arriving now from Asia and the Caribbean have access to public assistance not available in earlier years. Nonetheless, the newest arrivals are also damaged by poverty, and their children often leave school early to take low-wage jobs.

Government intervention, mostly nonexistent in the nineteenth and early twentieth centuries, has made a difference in the condition of families without resources because of the desertion or death of the breadwinner, exceeding the role played earlier by private organizations such as the Charity Organization Society and the Hebrew Orphan Asylum, to name only two. As a result of more generous allowances and the advances of medical knowledge, infant mortality rates are much lower; even the poorest of the newly arrived children can expect a longer lifespan. They are also expected to attend and remain in school for more years, and, most significant, their teachers no longer try to turn them into instant Americans. Unlike the experience of non-English-speaking children in the past, most of the foreign youngsters entering school today are placed in bilingual or ESL programs and study a multicultural curriculum.

These changes in educational theory and practice should relieve some of the pain of moving between cultures. The immigrant children of yesteryear were led to believe that the speech and traditions of their parents were inferior to the English language and that American history was more glorious than anything in the European past. Today immigrant children are taught to value and celebrate the achievements of non-American cultures, including their own. The new approaches have produced mixed results. Immigrant children today have less reason to feel marginal and more reason to feel enriched by being part of two cultures. They may also have more respect for their parents, whose language and traditions appear to be valued by educational authorities. This, in turn, should lessen the self-hatred that damaged so many immigrant children in bygone years.

There is, however, a downside to this new approach to education. In the past, when schools used "sink or swim" methods to teach English or laid on heavy Americanization, they failed to reach untold numbers of immigrant children who simply dropped out and went to work. Today, new methods and curricula, together with stronger child-labor laws, keep children in school longer, but when they graduate they are often ill equipped to meet the demands of modern American society. Perhaps this is too gloomy a con-clusion. Other changes, such as affirmative action, have diminished the effects of bigotry, and the presumed tenor of American life today is to respect cultural differences. Both trends may enable the immigrant children of the current generation—although they will not receive the more inclusive education offered to children who stayed in school in the past—to move into the middle class.

The future, to paraphrase an old song, is not ours to see. But writing from the vantage point of the mid-1990s, it appears that the nuclear family, a bulwark in the lives of immigrant children in the past, is no longer as strong an influence on youngsters in foreign families today. It is true that parents and children at other times did not see eye to eye on many issues, that fathers disappeared in years past as they do in the present, that child abuse was at least as prevalent then as it is now; but family attachments, per-haps born out of necessity, were stronger, as was religious observance. The weakening of both these ties is common to American society as a whole, but perhaps most damaging to children of immigrants, who—now as then—are likely to be susceptible to antisocial influences.

To end on a cheerful note, however, in spite of the hazards, known and unknown, it is a fact that more doors are open and fewer roads blocked for the immigrant children of today, which should help them become productive Americans in the future.

Notes

Chapter 1

1. Carl Wittke, *We Who Built America: The Saga of the Immigrant* (1939; Cleveland: Press of Case Western Reserve University, 1967), 6.
2. Ibid.; Samuel Morison and Henry Steele Commager, *The Growth of the American Republic* (New York: Oxford University Press, 1962), 1:502.
3. Gottlieb M. Helberger, "Journey to America in the Year 1750," in *The Way We Lived*, ed. Frederick Binder and David Reimers (Toronto: D. C. Heath, 1972), 32.
4. Wittke, *We Who Built America*, 10, 11, 86; Morison and Commager *American Republic*, 63.
5. Robert Divine, *America Past and Present* (New York: Scott Foresman, 1984), 1:91.
6. Morison and Commager, *American Republic*, 108, 76.
7. Wittke, *We Who Built America*, 439, xvi; Morison and Commager *American Republic*, 364.
8. Philip Taylor, *The Distant Magnet: European Emigration to the United States* (New York: Harper and Row, 1971), 133.
9. Robert Ernst, *Immigrant Life in New York* (Port Washington, N.Y.: Ira J. Friedman, 1948), 29; Taylor, *Distant Magnet*, 133, 137.
10. Francis Lane, "American Charities and the Child of the Immigrant, 1845–1880" (Ph.D. diss., Catholic University, 1932), 14–15; Taylor, *Distant Magnet*, 140.

11. Oscar Handlin, *Boston's Immigrants: A Study in Acculturation* (New York: Atheneum, 1968), 50; Taylor, *Distant Magnet,* 141.

12. Ernst, *Immigrant Life,* 29.

13. Ibid., 31.

14. Terry Coleman, *Going to America* (Garden City, N.Y.: Anchor Books, 1973), 267; Taylor, *Distant Magnet,* 126–27.

15. Lane, "American Charities," 25, 26.

16. Jay P. Dolan, *The Immigrant Church: New York's Irish and German Catholics, 1815–1865* (Baltimore: Johns Hopkins University Press, 1975) 135, 136.

17. Hyman Bogen, *The Luckiest Orphans: A History of the Hebrew Orphan Asylum of New York* (Urbana: University of Illinois Press, 1992), 19; Lane, "American Charities," 97, 105.

18. Gary E. Polster, *Inside, Looking Out: The Cleveland Jewish Orphan Asylum, 1898–1924* (Kent, Ohio: Kent State University Press, 1990), 59; Lane, "American Charities," 119–22.

19. Wittke, *We Who Built America,* 119–120

20. Eugene Boe, "Pioneers to Eternity," in *The Immigrant Experience,* ed. Thomas Wheeler (New York: Dial Press, 1971), 65, 76.

21. Theodore Blegen, *Norwegian Migration to America 1825–1860* (New York: Arno Press, 1969), 17, 127, 351, 367.

22. O. E. Rolvaag, *Giants in the Earth* (New York: Harper and Row, 1927), 38; Einar Haugen, *The Norwegians in America* (New York: Teachers College Press, 1967), 10.

23. Jerre Mangione and Ben Morreale, *La Storia: Five Centuries of the Italian American Experience* (New York: HarperCollins, 1992), 92.

24. Taylor, *Distant Magnet,* 151, 153; Sydelle Kramer and Jenny Masur, eds., *Grandmother's World* (Boston: Beacon Press, 1976), 93; interview with Lena W., 3 April 1985.

25. Steven Ascheim, *Brothers and Other Strangers: East European Jews in German and German Jewish Consciousness, 1880–1923* (Madison: University of Wisconsin Press, 1982), passim; interview with Sadie B., 20 April 1979.

26. Mary Antin, *The Promised Land* (Boston: Houghton Mifflin, 1969), 171, 174.

27. Taylor, *Distant Magnet,* 147, 149.

28. Sydney Stahl Weinberg, *Worlds of Our Mothers: Lives of Jewish Immigrant Women* (Chapel Hill: University of North Carolina Press, 1988), 67, 69.

29. Moses Rischin, *The Promised City: New York's Jews, 1870–1914* (Cambridge: Harvard University Press, 1962), 106; Thomas Pitkin, *Keepers of the Gate: A History of Ellis Island* (New York: New York University Press, 1975), 15.

30. Bertha Boody, *A Psychological Study of Immigrant Children at Ellis Island* (New York: Arno Press, 1970), 50; Taylor, *Distant Magnet,* 165.
31. Corrine A. Krause, *Grandmothers, Mothers, and Daughters: Oral Histories of Three Generations of Ethnic American Women* (Boston: Twayne Publishers, 1991), 128.
32. Boody, *Ellis Island,* 57.
33. Kramer and Masur, *Grandmother's World,* 128; Boody, *Ellis Island,* 103–4.
34. Pitkin, *Keepers,* 78.
35. Diane Mei Lin Mark and Ginger Chin, *A Place Called Chinese America* (New York: Organization of Chinese Americans, 1972), 34.
36. Thomas Kessner and Betty Boyd Caroli, *Today's Immigrants* (New York: Oxford University Press, 1982), 127, 135.
37. June Namias, *First Generation: In the Words of Twentieth-Century American Immigrants* (Boston: Beacon Press, 1978), 205; Kessner and Caroli, *Today's Immigrants,* 168.
38. Joan M. First, *New Voices: Immigrant Children in United States Public Schools* (Boston: National Coalition of Advocates for Students, 1985), 34, 31; Kessner and Caroli, *Today's Immigrants,* 135.
39. Ernst, *Immigrant Life,* 48, 49.
40. Wittke, *We Who Built America,* 134.
41. Ernst, *Immigrant Life,* 41–42.
42. Rolvaag, *Giants,* 23.
43. Hamlin Garland, *A Son of the Middle Border* (New York: Macmillan, 1962), 78.
44. Blegen, *Norwegian Migration,* 207.
45. Rischin, *Promised City,* 79; Deborah Dash Moore, *At Home in America: Second Generation New York's Jews* (New York: Columbia University Press, 1981), 20; Thomas Kessner, *The Golden Door: Italian and Jewish Immigrant Mobility in New York City* (New York: Oxford University Press, 1977), 129–30.
46. Rischin, *Promised City,* 83.
47. Harry Roskolenko, *The Time That Was Then: The Lower East Side, 1900–1914* (New York: Dial Press, 1971), 16–17; Jacob Riis, *The Children of the Poor* (New York: Charles Scribner's Sons, 1892), 39; Abraham Karp, *Golden Door to America* (New York: Penguin Books, 1977), 128.
48. Leonard Dinnerstein and David Reimers, *Uncertain Americans: A History of Immigration* (New York: Harper and Row, 1988), 54; Dale Steiner, *Of Thee I Sing: Immigrants and American History* (New York: Harcourt, Brace and Jovanovich, 1987), 181; Mangione and Morreale, *La Storia,* 145.
49. Maxwell Whiteman, "Philadelphia's Jewish Neighborhoods," in

Peoples of Philadelphia: A History of Ethnic Groups and Lower Class Life, 1790–1940, ed. Allen Davis and Mark Haller (Philadelphia: Temple University Press, 1973), 240, 242.

50. Elizabeth Ewen, *Immigrant Women in the Land of Dollars: Life and Customs on the Lower East Side, 1890–1925* (New York: Monthly Review Press, 1985), 152–53; quote from Lefkowitz on p. 153.

51. Rosemary Prosen, "Looking Back," in *Growing Up Slavic in America,* ed. Michael Novak (Bayville, N.Y.: EMPAC!, 1976), 5, 6; Harriet Pawlowska, "The Education of Harriet Pawlowska," in *Growing Up Slavic,* ed. Novak, 21–22.

52. First, *New Voices,* 28.

53. Rose Chao, *Chinese Immigrant Children* (Washington, D.C.: Department of Health, Education, and Welfare, 1977), 20, 21.

54. Marie Prisland, "Memories of an Old Wood Stove," in *The Ethnic American Woman: Problems, Protests, Lifestyle,* ed. Edith Blicksilver (Dubuque: Kendal/Hunt Publishing Co., 1978), 279; Roskolenko, *Time That Was,* 152.

55. William Alfred, "Pride and Poverty: An Irish Integrity," in *Immigrant Experience,* ed. Wheeler, 21; Handlin, *Boston's Immigrants,* 118; Carol Groneman, "The Bloody Ould Sixth: A Social Analysis of a New York City Working Class Community in Mid-Nineteenth Century" (Ph.D. diss., University of Rochester, 1973), 91, 93, 94.

56. "About a Wheat Field and a Bowl of Barley Porridge," in *Immigrant Women,* ed. Maxine Schwartz Seller (Philadelphia: Temple University Press, 1981), 28–29.

57. Jerre Mangione, *Mount Allegro: A Memoir of Italian-American Life* (New York: Columbia University Press, 1972), 222; interview with Salem J., 5 October 1991.

58. Burton Hendrick and Paul Kennaday, "Three Cent Lunches for School Children," *McClure's* 5 (October 1913): 124.

59. Parmatra Saran and Edwin Eames, *The New Ethnics: Asian Indians in the United States* (New York: Praeger Publishers, 1980), 212.

60. Prosen, "Looking Back," 5; Pawlowska, "Education," 21.

61. "The Vine and the Fruit," in *Immigrant Women,* ed. Seller, 146, 148.

62. Boe, "Pioneers to Eternity," 65; Thomas Christensen, *A History of the Danes in Iowa* (New York: Arno Press, 1979), 93.

63. Elliott West, "Children on the Plains Frontier," in *Small Worlds: Children and Adolescents in America, 1850–1950,* ed. Elliott West and Paula Petrik (Lawrence: University Press of Kansas, 1992), 308.

64. Ernst, *Immigrant Life,* 53; Donald Cole, *Immigrant City, Lawrence, Massachusetts, 1845–1920* (Chapel Hill: University of North Carolina Press, 1963), 106.

65. Handlin, *Boston's Immigrants,* 117; Samuel H. Preston and Michael R.

Haines, *Fatal Years: Child Mortality in Late Nineteenth-Century America* (Princeton: Princeton University Press, 1991), 99–101.

66. John Bodnar, *The Transplanted* (Bloomington: Indiana University Press, 1985), 77; Stanley Feldstein and Lawrence Costello, eds., *The Ordeal of Assimilation: A Documentary History of the White Working Class* (Garden City, N.Y.: Anchor Press, 1974), 227.

67. Interview with Lena K., 10 June 1962.

68. Virginia Yans-McLaughlin, *Family and Community: Italian Immigrants in Buffalo, 1880–1930* (Urbana: University of Illinois Press, 1982), 106, 167.

69. Maxine Schwartz Seller, *To Seek America: A History of Ethnic Life in the United States* (New York: Jerome Ozer, 1988), 130.

70. Nils Carpenter, *Immigrants and Their Children, Census Monograph VII* (Washington, D.C.: Government Printing Office, 1927), 245.

71. Dolan, *Immigrant Church*, 135–38; Handlin, *Boston's Immigrants*, 162.

72. Pyong Gap Min, "The Korean American Family," in *Ethnic American Families*, ed. Bernard Farber, Charles H. Mindel, and Roosevelt Wright, Jr. (New York: Elsevier, 1981), 209.

73. Cole, *Immigrant City*, 32, 196.

74. Ernst, *Immigrant Life*, 102.

75. Wittke, *We Who Built America*, 131–32, 206–7; Dinnerstein and Reimers, *Uncertain Americans*, 38.

76. Irving Howe, *World of Our Fathers*, (New York: Harcourt, Brace Jovanovich, 1976), 264.

77. Selma Berrol, *Immigrants at School* (New York: Arno Press, 1978), 87; interview with Shirley K., 24 June 1990.

78. Interview with Elaine T., 24 May 1991.

79. Moore, *At Home in America*, 37–38, 39.

80. Rischin, *Promised City*, 265.

81. Joseph Tait, *Some Aspects of the Effects of the Dominant Culture on the Children of Italian Born Parents* (Clifton, N.J.: Augustus M. Kelley, 1972), 50, 52; Blicksilver, *Ethnic American Woman*, 28; "Antonio Cardoso: Boy from the Azores," in *First Generation*, ed. Namias, 173.

82. Thomas Napierkowski, "Stepchild of America: Growing Up Polish," in *Growing Up Slavic*, ed. Novak, 14.

83. George Kennan, "The Japanese in the San Francisco Schools," *Outlook* 86 (June 1970): 247–52.

84. Mark and Chin, *Chinese America*, 75.

85. Nancy Foner, "New Immigrants and Changing Patterns in New York City," in *New Immigrants in New York*, ed. Nancy Foner (New York: Columbia University Press, 1987), 27.

86. Susan Buchanan Stafford, "The Haitians," in *New Immigrants*, ed. Foner, 151.

87. "This Is Selina," in *Immigrant Women,* ed. Seller, 307, 308.
88. Min, "Korean American Family," 255; Namias, *First Generation,* 215; First, *New Voices,* 25.
89. Morrison Wong, "The Ghetto and the Professional Chinese Family," in *Ethnic American Families,* ed. Farber, Mindel, and Wright, 245, 248.; Chao, *Chinese Immigrant Children,* 14; "The New Kids," *New York Times,* 17 July 1993, 32.
90. Roger Daniels, *Concentration Camps, USA* (New York: Holt, Rinehart, and Winston, 1971), 109.
91. Ibid., 110.
92. Namias, *First Generation,* 129.
93. Blicksilver, *Ethnic American Woman,* 331.

Chapter 2

1. Patricia Ferguson Clement, "The City and the Child, 1860–1885," in *American Childhood: A Research Guide and Historical Handbook,* ed. Joseph M. Hawes and N. Ray Hiner (Westport, Conn.: Greenwood Press, 1985), 242, 246.
2. Carl Kaestle, *Pillars of the Republic: Common Schools and American Society, 1780–1860* (New York: Hill and Wang, 1983), 98.
3. Dinnerstein and Reimers, *Uncertain Americans,* 60.
4. Diane Ravitch, *The Great School Wars, New York City, 1805–1973: A History of the Public Schools as Battlefield of Social Change* (New York: Basic Books, 1974), xiii, xiv, xv.
5. Handlin, *Boston's Immigrants,* 135.
6. Ravitch, *School Wars,* 37.
7. Ernst, *Immigrant Life,* 141.
8. Ibid.; Carl Kaestle, *Evolution of an Urban School System, New York City, 1750–1850* (Cambridge: Harvard University Press, 1973), 143–44.
9. Blicksilver, *Ethnic American Woman,* 310.
10. Joseph Lopreato, *Italian Americans* (New York: Random House, 1970), 83; Richard Varbero, "Philadelphia's South Italians in the 1920's," in *The Peoples of Philadelphia,* ed. Allen Davis and Mark Haller (Philadelphia: Temple University Press, 1973), 259; Richard Ulin, *The Italo-American Student in the American Public School* (New York: Arno Press, 1975), 146, 156.
11. John Bodnar, Roger Simon, and Michael Weber, eds., *Lives of Their Own: Blacks, Italians, and Poles in Pittsburgh, 1900–1960* (Urbana: University of Illinois, 1982), 96; Judith Smith, *Family Connections: A History of Italian and Jewish Immigrant Lives in Providence, Rhode Island, 1900–1948* (Albany: SUNY Press, 1985), 27.
12. Charles Churchill, *Italians of Newark: A Community Study* (New York: Arno Press, 1975), 153; Smith, *Family Connections,* 72.

13. Leonard Covello, *Social Background of the Italo-American School Child* (Totowa, N.J.: Roman and Littlefield, 1972), 289, 292; Gary Mormino, *Immigrants on the Hill: Italian Americans in St. Louis* (Urbana: University of Illinois Press, 1986), 33.

14. Mormino, *Immigrants on the Hill*, 109; Salvatore La Gumina, "American Education and the Italian Immigrant Response," in *American Education and the European Immigrant*, ed. Bernard Weiss (Urbana: University of Illinois Press, 1982), 68.

15. Bodnar, Simon, and Weber, *Lives of Their Own*, 93–94; Bodnar, *The Transplanted*, 195; Eugene Obidinski, *Ethnic to Status Group: A Study of Polish Americans in Buffalo* (New York: Arno Press, 1980), 84; Stanley Feldstein and Lawrence Costello, eds., *The Ordeal of Assimilation: A Documentary History of the White Working Class* (Garden City, N.Y.: Doubleday, 1974), 134.

16. Ewa Morawska, *For Bread and Butter: The Life World of East Central Europeans in Johnstown, Pennsylvania, 1890–1940* (Cambridge: Cambridge University Press, 1985), 244; Paul Wrobel, *Our Way: Family, Parish, and Neighborhood in a Polish American Community* (Notre Dame: University of Notre Dame Press, 1979), 77.

17. Smith, *Family Connections*, 72; John W. Briggs, *An Italian Passage: Immigrants in Three American Cities, 1890–1930* (New Haven: Yale University Press, 1978), 238, 241; Morawska, *For Bread and Butter*, 132, 133.

18. Josef Barton, *Peasants and Strangers: Italians, Rumanians, and Slovaks in an American City, 1890–1950* (Cambridge: Harvard University Press, 1975), 128, 133, 146.

19. Berrol, *Immigrants at School*, 274; Howe, *World of Our Fathers*, 275.

20. Selma Berrol, "Education and Economic Mobility: The Jewish Experience in New York City, 1880–1920," *American Jewish Historical Quarterly*, January 1976, passim.

21. Dinnerstein and Reimers, *Uncertain Americans*, 116, 117, 132.

22. Elizabeth Lopez Newby, "The Struggle for Higher Education," in *Immigrant Women*, ed. Seller, 222–27.

23. Leo Pap, *Portugese Americans* (Boston: Twayne Publishers, 1981), 116, 118.

24. Glenn Hendricks, *Dominican Diaspora: From the Dominican Republic to New York City, Villagers in Transition* (New York: Teachers College Press, 1974), 133, 134; Patricia R. Pessar, "The Dominican Women in the Household and Garment Industry," in *New Immigrants*, ed. Foner, 124.

25. Annaliese Orleck, "The Soviet Jews: Life in Brighton Beach, Brooklyn," in *New Immigrants*, ed. Foner, 285.

26. This statement is based on my experiences teaching introductory history courses at Baruch College, CUNY, since 1968. I have seen an

increasing number of students who are graduates of these programs, most of whom have only limited ability to read, write, and speak English.

27. Jade Snow Wong, "Puritans from the Orient: A Chinese Evolution," in *Immigrant Experience,* ed. Wheeler, 111.

28. Dolan, *Immigrant Church,* 113.

29. Kaestle, *Urban School System,* 142, 155.

30. New York Children's Aid Society, "Third Annual Report, 1856," in *Children and Youth in America: A Documentary History,* ed. Robert Bremner (Cambridge: Harvard University Press, 1970), 1:425–26.

31. Steven Hertzberg, *Strangers in the Gate City: Jews of Atlanta* (Philadelphia: Jewish Publication Society, 1978), 19.

32. Christensen, *History of the Danes in Iowa,* 146, 148.

33. Theodore Blegen, *Norwegian Migration to America, 1825–1860* (New York: Arno Press, 1969), 100, 179, 207.

34. Blicksilver, *Ethnic American Woman,* 164.

35. Selma Berrol, "Who Went to School," in *Essays in the History of New York City: A Memorial to Sydney Pomerantz,* ed. Irwin Yellowitz (Port Washington, N.Y.: Kennikat Press, 1978), 42.

36. U.S. Immigration Commission, *Abstract of the Report on the Children of Immigrants in the Schools* (Washington, D.C.: Government Printing Office, 1911), 1:8–13, 21.

37. Robert Woods, ed., *Americans in Process* (New York: Arno Press, 1970), 292; Berrol, *Immigrants at School,* 87.

38. Neil Cowan and Ruth Schwartz Cowan, *Our Parents' Lives* (New York: Basic Books, 1989), 86; Varbero, "Philadelphia's South Italians," 256.

39. Berrol, *Immigrants at School,* 106–7.

40. Woods, *Americans in Process,* 300–301.

41. Humbert S. Nelli, *Italians in Chicago, 1880–1930: A Study in Ethnic Mobility* (New York: Oxford University Press, 1970), 68; Churchill, *Italians of Newark,* 84.

42. La Gumina, "American Education," 69; Jerre Mangione, *Mount Allegro* (New York: Columbia University Press, 1972), 209.

43. Berrol, *Immigrants at School,* 57; Dorothy Reed, "Leisure Time of Girls in Little Italy" (Ph.D. diss., Columbia University, 1932), 32.

44. Grace Irwin, "Michaelangelo in Newark," *Harper's Monthly,* September 1921, 433.

45. Leonard Covello, *The Heart Is the Teacher* (New York: McGraw Hill, 1958), 25, 26.

46. Krause, *Grandmothers, Mothers, and Daughters,* 152, 153.

47. Cowan and Cowan, *Our Parents' Lives,* 87; Woods, *Americans in Process,* 291.

48. Cowan and Cowan, *Our Parents' Lives,* 88; Charles Ferroni, *Italians in Cleveland* (New York: Arno Press, 1969)), 232.

49. Berrol, *Immigrants at School,* 217–27.

50. Woods, *Americans in Process,* 293.

51. Ferroni, *Italians in Cleveland,* 214, 232.

52. Susan Glenn, *Daughters of the Shtetl: Life and Labor in the Immigrant Generation* (Ithaca: Cornell University Press, 1990), 167; New York City, Department of Education, "Fourth Annual Report of the City Superintendent of Schools, 1902," 29–30.

53. Seller, *To Seek America,* 127; Woods, *Americans in Process,* 298; Cowan and Cowan, *Our Parents' Lives,* 90.

54. Marie Richmond, *Immigrant Adaptation and Family Structures among Cubans in Miami, Florida* (New York: Arno Press, 1980), 44–45; Orleck, "Soviet Jews," 293.

55. Betty Lee Sung, *Transplanted Chinese Children* (Washington, D.C.: Department of Health, Education, and Welfare, 1979), 52, 53.

56. Instructional Resource Center, Office of Academic Affairs, City University of New York, "Into the Academic Mainstream: Guidelines for Teaching Language Minority Students," 1992, 1; Andrew T. Kopan, review of "Education and Greek Immigrants to Chicago," *Journal of American Ethnic History,* Fall 1992, 126.

57. "Immigrant Fear of Forms Imperils Aid to School," *New York Times,* 8 November 1992, 25.

58. Aubrey Bonnett, "Patterns of Accommodation in the West Indian Community of New York," in "Schooling, Job Opportunities, and Ethnic Mobility among Caribbean Youth in the United States," type-script of a paper delivered at a conference sponsored by Fordham University and ASPIRA in 1990, 45.

59. Thomas Muller and Thomas Espenshade, *Fourth Wave* (Washington, D.C.: Urban Institute Press, 1985), 80, 81.

60. Sung, *Transplanted Chinese Children,* 52, 53; Chao, *Chinese Immigrant Children,* 9–10, 12, 14; Henry Trueba, Lila Jacobs, and Elizabeth Kirton, *Culture Conflict and Adaptation: The Case of Hmong Children in American Society* (New York: Falner Press, 1990), 81.

61. First, *New Voices,* 20, 22, 23.

62. Ibid., 20.

63. Chao, *Chinese Immigrant Children,* 10.

64. First, *New Voices,* 43.

65. Chao, *Chinese Immigrant Children,* 25.

66. New York State United Teachers, *New York Teacher,* 14 June 1993, 13.

67. First, *New Voices,* 88, 104.

68. Berrol, *Immigrants at School,* 219.

69. Ibid., 220, 221.
70. Muller and Espenshade, *Fourth Wave,* 86.
71. Sung, *Transplanted Chinese Children,* 55.
72. First, *New Voices,* 53.
73. Handlin, *Boston's Immigrants,* 216–17.
74. Dolan, *Immigrant Church,* 105; William Alfred, "Pride and Poverty: An Irish Integrity," in *Immigrant Experience,* ed. Wheeler, 26; Joel Perlmann, *Ethnic Differences* (Cambridge: Cambridge University Press, 1988), 23; Woods, *Americans in Process,* 313.
75. Iris Saunders Podea, "Quebec to Little Canada," in *Uncertain Americans,* ed. Dinnerstein and Reimers, 177; Edith Abbott and Sophinisba Breckenridge, *Truancy and Nonattendance in the Chicago Schools* (Chicago: University of Chicago Press, 1917), 101, 351; Perlmann, *Ethnic Differences,* 23; Selwyn Troen, *The Public and the Schools* (Columbia: University of Missouri Press, 1975), 130.
76. U.S. Immigration Commission, *Children of Immigrants,* 1:14–19; Ravitch, *School Wars,* 244.
77. U.S. Immigration Commission, *Children of Immigrants,* 1:32, 33; Woods, *Americans in Process,* 297.
78. Abbott and Breckenridge, *Truancy,* 270.
79. Ibid., 267.
80. Paula S. Fass, *Outside In: Minorities and the Transformation of American Education* (New York: Oxford University Press, 1989), 43.
81. Berrol, *Immigrants at School,* 269, 270, 275; Ravitch, *School Wars,* 89.
82. Berrol, *Immigrants at School,* 287.
83. Woods, *Americans in Process,* 299.
84. Ibid., 315.
85. Abbott and Breckenridge, *Truancy,* 237, 274, 276; Sophinisba Breckenridge, *New Homes for Old* (New York: Harper and Bros., 1921), 232.
86. Perlmann, *Ethnic Differences,* 83; Barton, *Peasants and Strangers,* 162.
87. David Hogan, "Education and the Working Class," in *Education and the Immigrant,* ed. George Pozzetta (New York: Garland, 1991), 173; Michael Olneck and Marvin Lazerson, "School Achievement of Immigrant Children, 1900–1930," in *Education and the Immigrant,* ed. Pozzetta, 261.
88. Bodnar, *The Transplanted,* 193; Ulin, *Italo-American Student,* 42; Briggs, *Italian Passage,* 237; Covello, *Italo-American School Child,* 285; Churchill, *Italians of Newark,* 158; Mormino, *Immigrants on the Hill,* 194.
89. Thomas Sowell, *Essays and Data on American Ethnic Groups* (Washington, D.C.: Urban Institute Press, 1978), 119; Bodnar, *The Transplanted,* 196; Joseph Van Denburg, *Causes of the Elimination of*

Students in the Public Secondary Schools of New York City (New York: Teachers College Press, 1911, 37; Howe, *World of Our Fathers,* 277.

90. Philip Roth, "The Man in the Middle," *New York Times,* 10 October 1992, 21; Blicksilver, *Ethnic American Woman,* 235, 195–97.

91. Kramer and Masur, *Grandmother's World,* 97; Krause, *Grandmothers, Mothers, and Daughters,* 112, 114.

92. Bodnar, Simon, and Weber, *Lives of Their Own,* 96; Bodnar, *The Transplanted,* 193; U.S. Immigration Commission, *Children of Immigrants,* 1:31, 38.

93. Hogan, "Education and the Working Class," 183.

94. Harry L. Kitano, "The Japanese American Family," in *Ethnic American Families,* ed. Farber, Mindel, and Wright, 264.

95. "Hispanic Drop-Out Rate Stays High," *New York Times,* 13 January 1994.

96. Margaret Gibson and John Ogbu, *Minority Status and Schooling* (New York: Garland, 1991), 138.

97. Hendricks, *Dominican Diaspora,* 131.

Chapter 3

1. Handlin, *Boston's Immigrants,* 61; Cole, *Immigrant City,* 33, 105.

2. Bodnar, *The Transplanted,* 76; Bremner, *Children and Youth,* 1:398, 403, 433; John Cumbler, *Working Class Community in Industrial America: Work, Leisure, and Struggle in Two Industrial Cities, 1880–1930* (Westport, Conn.: Greenwood Press, 1979), 153–54.

3. Cumbler, *Working Class Community,* 105, 132, 134.

4. Wittke, *We Who Built America,* 139; Arthur Calhoun, *A Social History of the American Family from Colonial Times to the Present* (Cleveland: Arthur H. Clark Co., 1917), 1:55, 75, 140; Bremner, *Children and Youth,* 1:416.

5. Seller, *Immigrant Women,* 264; U.S. Congress, *Report on the Condition of Women and Child Wage Earners in the United States,* 61st Congress, 2d Session, Senate Document 645, vol. 4, 471.

6. Iris Saunders Podea, "Quebec to Little Canada," 177; Vivian Zelizer, *Pricing the Priceless Child* (New York: Basic Books, 1985), 68.

7. West, "Children on the Plains Frontier," 28.

8. Boe, "Pioneers to Eternity," 78.

9. John Bodnar, "Schooling and the Slavic-American Family, 1900–1940," in *American Education,* ed. Weiss, 76; Clement, "The City and the Child," 249.

10. Ewen, *Immigrant Women in the Land of Dollars,* 99; Smith, *Family Connections,* 60, 75.

11. Smith, *Family Connections,* 31; interview with Leah W., 3 April 1965; Hyman Cantor, "His Story" (unpublished autobiography at YIVO

Institute, New York City), 20; Feldstein and Costello, *Ordeal of Assimilation*, 255; Yans-McLaughlin, *Family and Community*, 54.

12. Bonnie Stepanoff, "Child Labor in the Pennsylvania Silk Mills: Protest and Change," *Pennsylvania History* 59 (April 1992): 109, 115.

13. Smith, *Family Connections*, 52; Thomas Kessner and Betty Boyd Caroli, "New Immigrants at Work," *Journal of American Ethnic Studies*, Winter 1978, 22.

14. Smith, *Family Connections*, 50, 52; Bremner, *Children and Youth*, 2:623.

15. Interview with Leah W., 3 April 1965; Abbott and Breckenridge, *Truancy*, 42.

16. Glenn, *Daughters of the Shtetl*, 72, 70–71.

17. Clement, "The City and the Child," 248; U.S. Immigration Commission, *Abstract of the Report on Immigrants in Cities* (Washington, D.C.: Government Printing Office, 1911), 42–43; Nelli, *Italians in Chicago*, 69–70.

18. U.S. Immigration Commission, *Immigrants in Cities*, 42; Perlmann, *Ethnic Differences*, 88.

19. Yans-McLaughlin, *Family and Community*, 190–97.

20. Ernst, *Immigrant Life*, 86; Woods, *Americans in Process*, 125; Bremner, *Children and Youth*, 1:400.

21. Glenn, *Daughters of the Shtetl*, 87; Ewen, *Immigrant Women in the Land of Dollars*, 125; Mangione and Morreale, *La Storia*, 145.

22. Reed, "Leisure Time," 29; Smith, *Family Connections*, 52–53; John Bodnar, "Schooling and the Slavic-American Family, 1900–1940," in *American Education*, ed. Weiss, 94.

23. Yans-McLaughlin, *Family and Community*, 53, 185, 191; Bremner, *Children and Youth*, 2:612, 623, 643–44.

24. Weinberg, *World of Our Mothers*, 192, 193.

25. Cowan and Cowan, *Our Parents' Lives*, 65.

26. Bremner, *Children and Youth*, 2:612, 623, 643–44.

27. Feldstein and Costello, *Ordeal of Assimilation*, 255, 259; Henry Fairchild, *Greek Immigration to the United States* (New Haven: Yale University Press, 1911), 172–73, 183.

28. Namias, *First Generation*, 33, 37; Smith, *Family Connections*, 27, 58.

29. Glenn, *Daughters of the Shtetl*, 86; Bodnar, "Schooling and the Slavic-American Family, 1900–1940," 82; Bremner, *Children and Youth*, 2:620.

30. Feldstein and Costello, *Ordeal of Assimilation*, 251; Woods, *Americans in Process*, 306.

31. Reed, "Leisure Time," 23; Glenn, *Daughters of the Shtetl*, 68; Zelizer, *Priceless Child*, 76.

32. Seller, *Immigrant Women,* 264.

33. Berrol, *Immigrants at School,* 273, 274, 275; A. E. Palmer, *History of the New York City Schools* (New York: Harper and Row, 1905), 181, 193, 227.

34. Fred S. Hall, *Forty Years, 1902–1942: The Work of the New York Child Labor Committee* (New York: New York Child Labor Committee, 1942), 47.

35. Abbott and Breckenridge, *Truancy,* 264; Bremner, *Children and Youth,* 2:612.

36. Albert Camarillo, *Chicanos in a Changing Society: From Mexican Pueblos to American Barrios in Santa Barbara and Southern California* (Cambridge: Harvard University Press, 1979), 166.

37. Wong, "Puritans from the Orient," 59.

38. Sung, *Transplanted Chinese Children,* 74.

39. *New York Times,* 14 October 1992, 59.

40. Clement, "The City and the Child," 235; David Nasaw, *Children of the City: At Work and Play* (Garden City, N.Y.: Anchor Press, 1985), 28, 109; Zelizer, *Priceless Child,* 35.

41. Zelizer, *Priceless Child,* 56; Harry Roskolenko, "America the Thief," in *Immigrant Experience,* ed. Wheeler, 76.

42. Cary Goodman, *Choosing Sides* (New York: Schocken Books, 1979), xiii.

43. Irving Howe and Kenneth Libo, *How We Lived* (New York: Richard Mark, 1979), 48; Nasaw, *Children of the City,* 19; Reed, "Leisure Time," 30–31, 44.

44. John Clark, "The Stoop Is the World," in *Growing Up in America,* ed. Joseph M. Hawes and N. Ray Hiner (Urbana: University of Illinois Press, 1965), 273; Mangione and Morreale, *La Storia,* 143; Nasaw, *Children of the City,* 18.

45. Howe and Libo, *How We Lived,* 48–49.

46. Howe, *World of Our Fathers,* 257–60; Suzanne Wasserman, "Cafés, Clubs, Corners, and Candy Stores: Youth, Leisure, and Culture on New York City's Lower East Side during the 1930's," *Journal of American Culture* 59 (April 1992): 43, 44, 45.

47. Goodman, *Choosing Sides,* 17, 22.

48. Nasaw, *Children of the City,* 32; Cowan and Cowan, *Our Parents' Lives,* 66; Goodman, *Choosing Sides,* 89.

49. Mario Puzo, "Choosing a Dream: Italians in Hell's Kitchen," in *Immigrant Experience,* ed. Wheeler, 40.

50. West, "Children on the Plains Frontier," 34.

51. Dominick Cavallo, *Muscles and Morals: Playgrounds and Urban Reform, 1898–1920* (Philadelphia: University of Pennsylvania Press, 1981), 23; Zelizer, *Priceless Child,* 34, 35.

52. Selma Berrol, *A Notable Woman: Julia Richman* (Cranbury, N.J.: Associated Universities Press, 1992), 96–97.
53. Sung, *Transplanted Chinese Children,* 112; Chao, *Chinese Immigrant Children,* 12.
54. Sung, *Transplanted Chinese Children,* 24; Chao, *Chinese Immigrant Children,* 31, 34, 35.
55. Wong, "Puritans from the Orient," 111.
56. Min, "Korean American Family," 220.
57. Roger Daniels, *Coming to America* (New York: HarperCollins, 1991), 368–70.

Chapter 4

1. Lawrence Brown, *Immigration* (New York: Longmans Green and Co., 1933), 254.
2. Ernst, *Immigrant Life,* 56.
3. Bogen, *The Luckiest Orphans,* 15, 18, 34.
4. Boe, "Pioneers to Eternity," 83; Alfred, "Pride and Poverty," 19; Blicksilver, *Ethnic American Woman,* 144, 153; Groneman, "The Bloody Ould Sixth," 53, 54, 57, 60, 66, 83–84.
5. Bodnar, *The Transplanted,* 72; John Bukowczyk, *And My Children Did Not Know Me: A History of Polish Americans* (Bloomington: Indiana University Press, 1987), 77; Yans-McLaughlin, *Family and Community,* 148; Smith, *Family Connections,* 24.
6. Smith, *Family Connections,* 56.
7. Bodnar, *The Transplanted,* 71–72, 75; Seller, *Immigrant Women,* 69.
8. Seller, *Immigrant Women,* 281.
9. Helena Lopata, "The Polish American Family," in *Ethnic American Families,* ed. Farber, Mindel, and Wright, 32.
10. D. Ann Squier and Jill S. Quadagno, "The Italian American Family," in *Ethnic American Families,* ed. Farber, Mindel, and Wright, 127; Yans-McLaughlin, *Family and Community,* 201; Lopreato, *Italian Americans,* 50–51, 58; Puzo, "Choosing a Dream," 47.
11. Cowan and Cowan, *Our Parents' Lives,* 196–97; George Kourvetaris, "The Greek American Family," in *Ethnic American Families,* ed. Farber, Mindel, and Wright, 87; Morris Rosenfeld in Abraham Karp, *Golden Door to America,* 133–34, poem originally published in R. J. Badge, *Songs of Labor and Other Poems,* trans. Rose Pastor Stokes and Helena Frank, 1914.
12. Wrobel, *Our Way,* 79, 83; Robert Foerster, *The Italian Immigration of Our Times* (Cambridge: Harvard University Press, 1924), 395; Steven Mintz and Susan Kellogg, *Domestic Revolution: A Social History of American Family Life* (New York: Free Press, 1988), 109–10.
13. Kourvetaris, "Greek American Family," 89; Helena Lopata, *Polish-*

Americans: Status Competition in an Ethnic Community (Englewood Cliffs, N.J.: Prentice-Hall, 1976), 100; Bernard Farber, Charles Mindel, and Robert W. Habenstein, "The Jewish American Family," in *Ethnic American Families,* ed. Farber, Mindel, and Wright, 426, 427; Blicksilver, *Ethnic American Woman,* 195; Isaac Metzger, ed., *A Bintel Brief: Sixty Years of Letters to the "Jewish Daily Forward"* (New York: Ballantine, 1971), 36.

14. Donald Tricarico, *Italians of Greenwich Village: Social Structure and Transformation of an Ethnic Community* (New York: Center for Migration Studies, 1984), 21.

15. Lopreato, *Italian Americans,* 63.

16. Rosina M. Becerra, "The Mexican American Family," in *Ethnic American Families,* ed. Farber, Mindel, and Wright, 141, 149, 156.

17. Hendricks, *Dominican Diaspora,* 131, 136; Benicio Catapusan, "The Social Adjustment of Filipinos in the United States" (Ph.D. diss., University of Southern California, 1940), 84.

18. Sung, *Transplanted Chinese Children,* 104; Wong, "Puritans from the Orient," 110–11; Morrison Wong, "The Chinese American Family," in *Ethnic American Families,* ed. Farber, Mindel, and Wright, 234, 238, 243; Seller, *Immigrant Women,* 124.

19. Forrest E. La Violette, *Americans of Japanese Ancestry: A Study of Assimilation in the American Community* (Toronto: Canadian Institute of International Affairs, 1945), 20, 21, 25.

20. Kitano, "Japanese American Family," 263; La Violette, *Japanese Ancestry,* 7.

21. Min, "Korean American Family," 215.

22. Saran and Eames, *New Ethnics,* 33, 34.

23. Marcus Lee Hansen, "The Third Generation," in *Children of the Uprooted,* ed. Oscar Handlin (New York: Grosset and Dunlap, 1968), 257–58.

24. Pauline Young, "Social Problems in the Education of the Immigrant Child," *American Sociological Review* 1 (1936): 419.

25. Jerre Mangione, "Talking American," in *Children of the Uprooted,* ed. Handlin, 221; Roskolenko, "America the Thief," 258.

26. Wasyl Halich, *Ukrainians in the United States* (Chicago: University of Chicago Press, 1937), dedication.

27. Young, "Social Problems," 426; Seller, *To Seek America,* 94.

28. Rivka Shpak Lissak, *Pluralism and Progressives: Hull House and the New Immigrants, 1890–1919* (Chicago: University of Chicago Press, 1989), 50; Julia Richman, "Immigrant Child," *Proceedings of the National Education Association, 1904,* 115.

29. Mangione and Morreale, *La Storia,* 222.

30. Feldstein and Costello, *Ordeal of Assimilation,* 365, 397.

31. Pawlowska, "Education," 22.
32. Interview with Shirley K., 24 June 1965; Krause, *Grandmothers, Mothers, and Daughters,* 24.
33. Mangione, "Talking American," 356; John Fante, "The Odyssey of a Wop," in *Children of the Uprooted,* ed. Handlin, 395; Samuel Ornitz, *Haunch, Paunch, and Jowl* (New York: Boni and Liverwright, 1923), 30.
34. Covello, *The Heart Is the Teacher,* 30–31.
35. Foerster, *Italian Immigration,* 409; Weinberg, *World of Our Mothers,* 114.
36. Pawlowska, "Education," 25; Prosen, "Looking Back," 2, 3.
37. Feldstein and Costello, *Ordeal of Assimilation,* 399; Krause, *Grandmothers, Mothers, and Daughters,* 35; Weinberg, *World of Our Mothers,* 111–12.
38. Kitano, "Japanese American Family," 271–72.
39. Namias, *First Generation,* 129, 130.
40. John Connor, *Tradition and Change in Three Generations of Japanese Americans* (Chicago: Nelson-Hall, 1977), 309.
41. Alexjandro Portes and Ruben Rumbaut, *Immigrant America: A Portrait* (Berkeley: University of California Press, 1990), 181; Catapusan, "Social Adjustment of Filipinos," 85; Michel Laguerre, *American Odyssey: Haitians in New York City* (Ithaca: Cornell University Press, 1984), 61.
42. Sung, *Transplanted Chinese Children,* 104.
43. Maxine Hong Kingston, "A Song for a Barbarian Reed Pipe," in *Immigrant Women,* ed. Seller, 290–91.
44. James Loewen, *Mississippi Chinese: Between Black and White* (Cambridge: Harvard University Press, 1971), 71, 82, 160, 161.
45. Orleck, "Soviet Jews," 293, 294, 295, 296.
46. Ibid., 294, 295.
47. Kourvetaris, "Greek American Family," 94; Hansen, "Third Generation," 258; Lissak, *Pluralism and Progressives,* 64, 71–73.
48. Dino Cinel, *From Italy to San Francisco: The Immigrant Experience* (Stanford: Stanford University Press, 1982), 124–26; Reed, "Leisure Time," 31.
49. Robert Kutak, *The Story of a Bohemian American Village* (New York: Arno Press, 1970), 84, 86; John Kolehmainen, *Finns in America* (New York: Teachers College Press, 1968), 37.
50. Namias, *First Generation,* 166; Weinberg, *World of Our Mothers,* 133; Foerster, *Italian Emigration,* 395.
51. Breckenridge, *New Homes for Old,* 170–71; Ewen, *Immigrant Women in the Land of Dollars,* 96.
52. Kramer and Masur, *Grandmother's World,* 130; Feldstein and

Costello, *Ordeal of Assimilation,* 364; Stephan Brumberg, "Going to School," in *Education and the Immigrant,* ed. Pozzetta, 120.

53. Cinel, *Italy to San Francisco,* 126, 129.

54. Hutchins Hapgood, *Spirit of the Ghetto* (New York: Funk and Wagnall, 1902), 26–27; Roskolenko, "America the Thief," 154.

55. Morawska, *For Bread and Butter,* 131; Weinberg, *World of Our Mothers,* 145; Breckenridge, *New Homes for Old,* 172.

56. Interview with Lena W., 7 June 1971; interview with Hyman K., 12 September 1958.

57. Morawska, *For Bread and Butter,* 77; Cinel, *Italy to San Francisco,* 129; Roskolenko, *Time That Was,* 34.

58. Weinberg, *World of Our Mothers,* 130; Fante, "Odyssey of a Wop," 393; Bodnar, Simon, and Weber, *Lives of Their Own,* 90.

59. Sung, *Transplanted Chinese Children,* 136; Wong, "Chinese American Family," 258; Chao, *Chinese Immigrant Children,* passim.

60. Connor, *Three Generations of Japanese Americans,* 183–89; Daniels, *Concentration Camps, USA,* 110.

61. Min, "Korean American Family," 219; Saran and Eames, *New Ethnics,* 212.

62. Dinnerstein and Reimers, *Uncertain Americans,* 192.

63. Orleck, "Soviet Jews," 294.

64. Laguerre, *Haitians in New York City,* 77.

65. Richmond, *Immigrant Adaptation,* 13, 168, 170–72; José Szapocznik and Roberto Hernandez, "The Cuban American Family," in *Ethnic American Families,* ed. Farber, Mindel, and Wright, 168–69.

66. William Thomas and Florian Znaniecki, *Polish Peasant in America* (Chicago: University of Chicago Press, 1918), 165.

67. Bremner, *Children and Youth,* 1:398, 400, 401, 416, 417.

68. Ibid., 421.; Joseph M. Hawes, *Children in Urban Society: Juvenile Delinquency in Nineteenth Century America* (New York: Oxford University Press, 1971), 94.

69. Alfred, "Pride and Poverty," 26, 28; Ellen Somers Horgan, "The American Catholic Irish Family," in *Ethnic American Families,* ed. Farber, Mindel, and Wright, 60, 61.

70. Boe, "Pioneers to Eternity," 83.

71. Tricarico, *Italians of Greenwich Village,* 21–22; interview with Doris P., 19 September 1989.

72. Squier and Quadagno, "Italian American Family," 126.

73. Yans-McLaughlin, *Family and Community,* 255; Harvey Zorbaugh, *The Gold Coast and the Slum: A Sociological Study of Chicago's Near North Side* (Chicago: University of Chicago Press, 1930), 154; Churchill, *Italians of Newark,* 84–85; Hawes, *Children in Urban Society,* 141.

74. Hawes, *Children in Urban Society,* 160–61.

75. Wasserman, "Cafés, Clubs, Corners, and Candy Stores," 45; Brecken-
    ridge, *New Homes for Old,* 185; Howe, *World of Our Fathers,* 263.
76. Helen S. Zand, "Polish Family Folkways in the United States," *Polish
    American Studies* 13 (1955): 88; Puzo, "Choosing a Dream," 38.
77. Sung, *Transplanted Chinese Children,* 136.
78. Hendricks, *Dominican Diaspora,* 142; Richmond, *Immigrant
    Adaptation,* 175.

Bibliographic Essay

To the best of my knowledge, prior to this publication, no book that focuses on the many different groups of immigrant children who have come to the United States had been written. When planning the research for this book, therefore, there was no standard work to which I could turn. As a result, I collected data from works on immigration and from studies on children and families, while noting the places where the two kinds of information intersected. The essay that follows reflects the results of this search. In this discussion of sources for a book on immigrant children, I move from the general to the particular without regard to chronology until I begin to describe materials about specific groups. At this point, I discuss the books and articles according to the order of arrival of the group with which they are concerned. I diverge from this pattern when collections, reminiscences, and autobiographies are described.

To begin with, several general texts on American immigration history are valuable, partly because they supply information on the subject of immigrant children and partly because their bibliographies lead to other sources. For the first purpose, I found Carl Wittke's *We Who Built America: The Saga of the Immigrant* (1939; Cleveland: Press of Case Western Reserve University, 1967) to be essential for the earliest periods of immigration. Philip Taylor's *The Distant Magnet: European Emigration to the United States* (New York: Harper and Row, 1971) is an excellent source for the transatlantic journey taken by European emigrants and their children, and John Bodnar's *The Transplanted* (Bloomington: Indiana University Press,

1985) is a good survey that reflects more recent scholarship. This is also true for Maxine Schwartz Seller's *To Seek America: A History of Ethnic Life in the United States* (New York: Jerome Ozer, 1988) and especially so for Roger Daniels's *Coming to America* (New York: HarperCollins, 1991).

My second step was to go to specialized studies likely to contain information on immigrant children. I found many to be useful, among them Arthur Calhoun's *A Social History of the American Family from Colonial Times to the Present,* vol. 1 (Cleveland: Arthur H. Clark Co., 1917), which, although old-fashioned, was useful for the colonial period and for information on Irish immigrant children who arrived during the famine years. John Cumbler's monograph *Working Class Community in Industrial America: Work, Leisure, and Struggle in Two Industrial Cities, 1880–1930* (Westport, Conn.: Greenwood Press, 1979) was of great value for its information on Irish, Portuguese, and French Canadian child laborers in Fall River, Massachusetts, between 1880 and 1930. Bonnie Stepanoff's article "Child Labor in the Pennsylvania Silk Mills: Protest and Change," which appeared in *Pennsylvania History* 59 (April 1992), added new information on immigrant children in the workplace.

Other examples of work on specialized topics that affected immigrant children would be Diane Ravitch's *The Great School Wars, New York City, 1805–1973* (New York: Basic Books, 1974), my own *Immigrants at School* (New York: Arno Press, 1978), Thomas Kessner's *The Golden Door: Italian and Jewish Immigrant Mobility in New York City* (New York: Oxford University Press, 1977), Stephan Brumberg's *Going to America, Going to School* (New York: Praeger Press, 1986), and Pauline Young's "Some Problems in the Education of the Immigrant Child," *American Sociological Review* 1 (1936). All focus on the largest immigrant-receiving city, New York. Ravitch was concerned with the battle over public schools when Irish children were involved and with the later battle involving Jewish and Italian immigrants; Kessner examined the intergenerational mobility of the latter two groups; Young addressed the difficulties the children faced. My own book focuses on the changes made by the school officials to accommodate the new arrivals as well as on the adjustments required of the youngsters and their parents.

Other materials, although not specifically focused on immigrant children, added a cheerful dimension to their often sad story. Some of these deal with city children at play, such as Dominick Cavallo's *Muscles and Morals: Playgrounds and Urban Reform, 1898–1920* (Philadelphia: University of Pennsylvania Press, 1981); John Clark's "The Stoop Is the World," part of Joseph M. Hawes and N. Ray Hiner's collection *Growing Up in America* (Urbana: University of Illinois Press, 1965); David Nasaw's *Children of the City: At Work and Play* (Garden City, N.Y.: Anchor Press, 1985); Cary Goodman's *Choosing Sides* (New York: Schocken Books, 1979); and Vivian Zelizer's *Pricing the Priceless Child* (New York: Basic Books, 1985). Still other works focus on the dark side of childhood. These include Robert Griswold, "Ties that Bind and Bonds that Break: Children's Attitudes toward Fathers," in Elliott West and Paula Petrik, *Small Worlds: Children and Adolescents in America, 1850–1950* (Lawrence: University of Kansas Press, 1992), and Samuel H. Preston and Michael R. Haines, *Fatal Years: Child Mortality in Late Nineteenth-Century America* (Princeton: Princeton University Press, 1991).

Several books that reflect the views of reformers active during different periods of heavy immigration provided information on various facets of the immigrant child's experience. Some of the most useful were Rivka Shpak Lissak's study of Hull House, *Pluralism and Progressives* (Chicago: University of Chicago Press, 1989); Francis Lane's dissertation, "American Charities and the Child of the Immigrant, 1845–1880," done at the Catholic University in 1932 and published by Arno Press in 1970; and *Americans in Process,* edited by Robert Woods, a collection of documents and essays written by settlement workers about the immigrant children who settled in the South End of Boston, also published by Arno Press in 1970. Most useful was Robert Bremner's *Children and Youth in America: A Documentary History* (Cambridge: Harvard University Press, 1970), a collection of documents and essays about children, many of which are connected to the experience of immigration.

Woods's collection was originally published in 1903 and thus reflects the work of the Progressives of that era. This is also true for Fred Hall's *Forty Years* (New York: Child Labor Committee, 1942), a description of the work of the New York City Child Labor Committee, written by the man who was its secretary from the committee's inception in 1902 to 1942. Other matters connected to immigrant children of concern to reformers at the turn of the century are reflected in Sophinisba Breckenridge's *New Homes for Old* (New York: Harper and Bros., 1921) and, more specifically, in *Truancy and Nonattendance in the Chicago Schools,* which she coauthored with another Chicago social service worker, Edith Abbott (Chicago: University of Chicago Press, 1917). At almost the same time, 1915, Elizabeth Irwin wrote a pamphlet, also titled *Truancy,* for the Public Education Association of New York. As described in my biography of Julia Richman, *A Notable Woman* (Cranbury, N.J.: Associated Universities Press, 1992), the main reason for concern over truancy was that it reduced the efficacy of the Americanization process, a major Progressive concern.

Several useful books compare immigrant groups without focusing primarily on children. One is Robert Ernst's *Immigrant Life in New York* (Port Washington, N.Y.: Ira J. Friedman, 1948). It is as much descriptive as comparative, but in any case it contains valuable information on the Irish and Germans who came to New York in the middle of the nineteenth century. Joel Perlmann's comparative study, *Ethnic Differences,* which looks at

Italians and Jews in Providence, Rhode Island, between 1880 and 1935 (Cambridge: Cambridge University Press, 1988), although quite different in approach (Perlmann's work is heavily statistical, Ernst's much less so), is also a notable contribution to the field of immigration history. The previously mentioned study by Thomas Kessner, *The Golden Door*, combines the best features of Perlmann and Ernst. Kessner used data from the New York State Census of 1905 and 1915 to compare the paths taken by Italian and Jewish immigrants in New York. Emulating Kessner and Perlmann is Judith Smith in her investigation *Family Connections: A History of Italian and Jewish Immigrant Lives in Providence, Rhode Island 1900–1948* (Albany: SUNY Press, 1985).

Studies of individual ethnic groups have proliferated in the last three decades. Much has been done on the Irish. To begin with there is Oscar Handlin's *Boston's Immigrants: A Study in Acculturation* (New York: Atheneum, 1968), which describes the difficult adjustment of the Catholic Irish in a Protestant city. Their experience in New York City was explored by Jay Dolan in *The Immigrant Church: New York's Irish and German Catholics, 1815–1865* (Baltimore: Johns Hopkins University Press, 1975), while Hasia Diner focused on Irish women in *Erin's Daughters in America* (Baltimore: Johns Hopkins University Press, 1983). James Sanders studied the Irish experience with schooling in Chicago in *Education of an Urban Minority* (New York: Oxford University Press, 1977), and Carol Groneman's dissertation on "The Bloody Ould Sixth," done at the University of Rochester in 1973, continues to be an extremely valuable source on the Irish community in Lower Manhattan. Ellen Somers Horgan's study "The American Catholic Irish Family," which appears in *Ethnic American Families*, edited by Bernard Farber, Charles Mindel, and Roosevelt Wright, Jr. (New York: Elsevier, 1981), contains other useful material.

An old but still available novel, *Giants in the Earth*, by O. E. Rolvaag (New York: Harper and Row, 1927), is well worth reading for information about Scandinavian immigrants. This is also true of Theodore Blegen's *Norwegian Migration to America* (New York: Arno Press, 1969). Somewhat newer is one of the few books written about Danish immigrants, Thomas Christensen's *History of the Danes in Iowa* (New York: Arno Press, 1979). An even greater rarity, a work on the Finns, is John Kolehmainen's *Finns in America* (New York: Teachers College Press, 1968).

Other European groups, such as those who came to the United States from Central Europe, have been investigated by John Bodnar in *The Transplanted* and by Ewa Moraskawa in *For Bread and Butter* (Cambridge: Cambridge University Press, 1985); the latter deals with Central Europeans who settled in Johnstown, Pennsylvania. Robert Kutak's *Story of a Bohemian American Village* (New York: Arno Press, 1970) discusses the Czechs who settled in a Nebraska village. An extremely valuable pamphlet edited by Michael Novak, *Growing Up Slavic in America* (Bayville, N.Y.: EMPAC!,

1976), contains essays written by the children of immigrants who came from Hungary and Poland, among other areas of Central Europe. Paul Wrobel's book *Our Way* (Notre Dame: University of Notre Dame Press, 1979) has useful information on one group of Slavic immigrants, the Poles. Other reliable studies of this group include Helena Lopata's "Polish American Families," in Farber, Mindel, and Wright's *Ethnic American Families;* Eugene Obidinski's *Ethnic to Status Group: A Study of Polish Americans in Buffalo* (New York: Arno Press, 1980); Paul Fox's *Poles in America* (New York: George H. Doran Co., 1922); and another old but still reliable work, William Thomas and Florian Znaniecki's *Polish Peasant in America* (Chicago: University of Chicago Press, 1918).

Regarding Jews, the following works are important: Moses Rischin's *The Promised City: New York's Jews, 1870–1914* (Cambridge: Harvard University Press, 1962), which deals with Jewish immigrants in New York; William Toll's study of the Jewish community in Portland, Oregon, *The Making of an Ethnic Middle Class* (Albany: SUNY Press, 1982); Steven Hertzberg's *Strangers in the Gate City* (Philadelphia: Jewish Publication Society, 1978), on the Jews who settled in Atlanta; and Stuart Rosenberg's *Jewish Community in Rochester* (New York: Columbia University Press, 1954).

Italians have been much studied. The many works available include John W. Briggs's *An Italian Passage: Immigrants in Three American Cities, 1890–1930* (New Haven: Yale University Press, 1978), Charles Churchill's *The Italians of Newark* (New York: Arno Press, 1975), Leonard Covello's *Social Background of the Italo-American School Child* (Totowa, N.J.: Roman and Littlefield, 1972), and Charles Ferroni's *Italians in Cleveland* (New York: Arno Press, 1969). Robert Foerster's *Italian Immigration of Our Times* (Cambridge: Harvard University Press, 1924) is a classic, and Virginia Yans-McLaughlin's *Family and Community* (Urbana: University of Illinois Press, 1982), which deals with the Italians who settled in Buffalo, is a well-known revisionist study of Italian family life. Joseph Lopreato's *Italian Americans* (New York: Random House, 1970) is a useful survey because it looks at the Italian experience nationwide. Gary Mormino's *Immigrants on the Hill* (Urbana: University of Illinois Press, 1986) is equally useful because it focuses on an Italian American community about which little has been written, that in St. Louis, Missouri. This segment would not be complete without mention of Humbert S. Nelli's *Italians in Chicago, 1880–1930* (New York: Oxford University Press, 1970) and of Jerre Mangione and Ben Morreale's valuable *La Storia: Five Centuries of the Italian American Experience* (New York: HarperCollins, 1992).

Chinese immigrants have had their misfortunes and successes recounted by Rose Chao in *Chinese Immigrant Children* (Washington, D.C.: Department of Health, Education, and Welfare, 1977), by Betty Lee Sung in *Transplanted*

Chinese Children (Washington, D.C.: Department of Health, Education, and Welfare, 1979), and by Francis Hsu in *The Challenge of the American Dream* (Belmont, Calif.: Wadsworth Publishing Co., 1971). Important contributions on Japanese American children are Reginald Bell's "Public School Education of Second Generation Japanese Children in California," appearing in Stanford University's Publications University Series 1, no. 3 (1935); Forrest La Violette's *Americans of Japanese Ancestry* (Toronto: Canadian Institute of International Affairs, 1945); and John Connor's *Tradition and Change in Three Generations of Japanese Americans* (Chicago: Nelson-Hall, 1977). Harry Kitano's "The Japanese American Family," in Farber, Mindel, and Wright's *Ethnic American Families,* is also useful.

A valuable study of East Asian Indians who have come to the United States appears in Parmatra Saran and Edwin Eames's *New Ethnics: Asian Indians in the United States* (New York: Praeger Publishers, 1980). One of the relatively rare works on one particular group of Asian Americans, the Filipinos, is Benicio Catapusan's dissertation "Social Adjustment of Filipinos in the United States," done at the University of Southern California at Los Angeles in 1940. It is also quite useful. Even less work has been done on Korean Americans, which makes Pyong Gap Min's "The Korean American Family," in *Ethnic American Families,* important.

More research and writing has been done on Hispanic immigrants from the Caribbean, Central America, and Mexico. Among the most useful studies are Thomas Muller and Thomas Espenshade's *Fourth Wave* (Washington, D.C.: Urban Institute Press, 1985); Rosina Becerra's "The Mexican American Family," in *Ethnic American Families;* and Albert Camarillo's *Chicanos in a Changing Society* (Cambridge: Harvard University Press, 1979). Glenn Hendricks has discussed the *Dominican Diaspora* (New York: Teachers College Press, 1974), Michel Laguerre the Haitian struggle in New York City in *American Odyssey* (Ithaca: Cornell University Press, 1984). Marie Richmond's *Immigrant Adaptation and Family Structure among Cubans in Miami, Florida* (New York: Arno Press, 1980), gives a complete picture of a group that has had tremendous impact on southern Florida. José Szapocznik and Roberto Hernandez supply more recent information on the intergenerational adjustments of this group in "The Cuban American Family," in *Ethnic American Families.*

To a greater extent than might be true in other historical subdisciplines, immigration historians have produced a large number of collected essays and articles, some original and some reprints, many of which contain discussions important to the history of immigrant children. Two of the best have already been cited: Hawes and Hiner's *Growing Up in America* and Farber, Mindel, and Wright's *Ethnic American Families.* Others that proved useful include George Pozzetta's *Education and the Immigrant* (New York: Garland Publishers, 1991), Thomas Wheeler's *Immigrant Experience* (New York: Dial

Press, 1971), Elliott West and Paul Petrik's *Small Worlds,* Bernard Weiss's *American Education and the European Immigrant* (Urbana: University of Illinois Press, 1982), John Bodnar, Roger Simon, and Michael Weber's *Lives of Their Own: Blacks, Italians, and Poles in Pittsburgh, 1900–1960* (Urbana: University of Illinois Press, 1982), and Maxine Schwartz Seller's *Immigrant Women* (Philadelphia: Temple University Press, 1981).

Several collections of Jewish reminiscences are valuable for their information on children's experiences, feelings, and attitudes. Noteworthy are Susan Glenn's *Daughters of the Shtetl* (Ithaca: Cornell University Press, 1990), Neil Cowan and Ruth Schwartz Cowan's *Our Parents' Lives* (New York: Basic Books, 1989), Elizabeth Ewen's *Immigrant Women in the Land of Dollars: Life and Customs on the Lower East Side, 1890–1925* (New York: Monthly Review Press, 1985), Sydelle Kramer and Jenny Masur's *Grandmother's World* (Boston: Beacon Press, 1976), Paula Hyman and Steven Chon's *The Jewish Family* (New York: Holmes and Meier, 1986), and Irving Howe and Kenneth Libo's *How We Lived* (New York: Richard Marek, 1979). Howe is also the author of the memoir *World of Our Fathers* (New York: Harcourt, Brace, Jovanovich, 1976).

Some immigrant children wrote full-length autobiographies once they grew up. Making allowances for the fact that memory is affected by the passage of time, these works add interesting details to the story of immigrant children. Among the many in print are Mary Antin's *The Promised Land* (Boston: Houghton Mifflin, 1969), Leonard Covello's *The Heart Is the Teacher* (New York: McGraw Hill, 1958), Samuel Ornitz's *Haunch, Paunch, and Jowl* (New York: Boni and Liverwright, 1923), and Harry Roskolenko's *When I Was Last on Cherry Street* (New York: Stein and Day, 1965).

Two books that deal with the experiences of immigrants and their children at Ellis Island deserve mention. They are Thomas Pitkin's *Keepers of the Gate* (New York: New York University Press, 1975) and Bertha Boody's *Psychological Study of Immigrant Children at Ellis Island* (New York: Arno Press, 1970). There are also several useful government publications resulting from the work of the U.S. Immigration Commission (1908–11). They include *The Abstract of the Report on Immigrants in Cities* and *The Abstract of the Report on the Children of Immigrants in the Schools.* Another important government publication, *Immigrants and Their Children,* was compiled by Nils Carpenter and published by the Bureau of the Census in 1920.

As is clear from this essay, as well as from the endnotes, some ethnic groups have been better represented in print than others, either because they have had more to say about themselves or because others have found more to say about them. Some of the most recent arrivals have not been here long enough to have much of an American history. Keeping this in mind, I have tried to give equal time whenever possible.

Index

The Author

Selma Cantor Berrol has been a professor of American history, teaching at Baruch College, CUNY, for nearly three decades. She holds a B.A. from Hunter College, an M.A. from Columbia University, and a Ph.D. from the City University of New York Graduate Center. She is the author of five books and numerous articles on the subject of immigrants and education.